VENICE

By the staff of Editions Berlitz

Revised edition 1981

Preface

A new kind of travel guide for the jet age. Berlitz has packed all you need to know about Venice into this compact and colourful book, one of an extensive series on the world's top tourist areas.

Like our phrase books and dictionaries, this book fits your pocket—in both size and price. It also aims to fit your travel needs:

- It concentrates on your specific destination—Venice—not an entire country.

- It combines easy reading with fast facts; what to see and do, where to shop, what to eat.

- An authoritative A-to-Z "blueprint" fills the back of the book, giving clear-cut answers to all your questions, from "What does it cost to rent a gondola?" to "How do I make a phone call?" plus how to get there and when to go and what to budget for.

- Easy-to-read maps in full colour of the major areas in and around Venice pinpoint sights you'll want to see.

In short, this handy guide will help you enjoy your trip to Venice. From the bustle of the Rialto to the sleepy charm of Burano, from riding the *vaporetto* to sampling Venice's art treasures—Berlitz tells you clearly and concisely what it's all about.

Let your travel agent help you choose a hotel. Let a restaurant guide help you choose a good place to eat. But to decide "What should we do today?" travel with Berlitz.

Area Specialist: Don Larrimore
Photography: Daniel Vittet
We're particularly grateful to the Italian Tourist Office in Venice for its assistance in the preparation of this guide.
Cartography: Falk-Verlag, Hamburg.

Contents

Maps: Bird's-Eye View of Venice pp. 6–7, Venetian Republic in the Mid-16th Century p. 19, Vaporetto Routes p. 25, San Marco p. 33, Venice–Centre pp. 54–55, Islands Surrounding Estuary p. 75.
Photos: pp. 2–3, Doges' Palace.

How to use this guide
If time is short, look for items to visit which are printed in bold type in this book, e.g. **Scala d'Oro.** Those sights most highly recommended are not only given in bold type but also carry our traveller symbol, e.g. **Piazza San Marco.**

Venice and the Venetians

Like a glistening gem on a cushion of blue, she lies curled there in her lagoon, serene in the knowledge of her special place in the sun. Venice is, and has always been, a city apart, a unique blend of West and East, not totally European or even Italian; traces of Byzantium and more distant oriental influence appear everywhere. It's all unlikely—and delightful.

Although the city fairly reeks of history and bustles with contemporary commerce, it somehow seems artificial, unreal, a fairy tale. Can people have lived in those incredibly ornate palaces? Can a city really function if its "streets are filled with water"?

Understandably, modesty is not a local virtue: "Venice, Queen of the Sea" and "Heart of the World" are slogans dating from the republic's heyday. Centuries later, this preeminently narcissistic city continues to marvel at her glories.

Few object when Venetians insist their city is the most beautiful in the world. It's unquestionably the quietest, thanks to the streets of water where buses, cars and motorscooters never pass. Whereas other cities possess artistic treasures, Venice *itself* is the treasure.

When the bright sun shines, as it does for some eight

months of the year, there's little indication of a melancholy Venice. If anybody's brooding about death or fiendishly conniving, it's hard to imagine why. In fact, now that the city has stopped sinking* and plans are finally underway to deal with the perils of flooding and pollution, there's less cause for gloom than there has been for decades.

The Venetian atmosphere is quite unlike that of ordinary cities. With so many narrow alleyways and bridges, certain

* A ten-year campaign to replace the artesian wells in and around Venice with aqueducts has had some promising results. It seems that an underground cushion of water has been built up again and Venice has stopped sinking. Now plans are being studied for ways to control the high tides which regularly inundate the city, eating away the foundations of Venice.

etiquette has to be observed—shoving and jostling discouraged, polite smiles encouraged. Everywhere you come in contact with human beings, with no escape into a car. Outdoors, people are always talking to friends or strangers, frequently negotiating business deals while strolling. Without wheeled transport, the pace of life in Venice is slower, and with so much beauty to gaze at, idleness seems quite acceptable.

This supremely improbable city rests on an archipelago of 118 flat islets, her buildings supported by countless millions of larch poles driven into the sediment. Fewer than 95,000 Venetians live here today, but at times there were

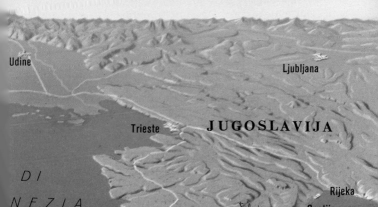

twice as many inhabitants.

The city is comprised of six districts, or *sestieri*, and subdivided into 33 parishes *(parrocchie)*—each a small village with a distinctive flavour.

Criss-crossing Venice are 177 canals spanned by 450 bridges, about 50 of them privately built and owned (nobles had to get into their palaces). The canals are partly flushed out by the tides that sweep in daily from the Adriatic through three seaways which pierce the ring of sand bars *(lidi)* protecting the lagoon.

The fortunes of Venice have always been linked with the sea from which she "sprang". For some eight centuries, until Napoleon abolished the republic, the doge of Venice sailed out to the Lido seaway in a magnificent galley every year on Ascension Day. Behind him came gondolas carrying all the city's notables. With the words, "We wed thee, sea, in token of our perpetual rule", the doge threw a golden ring into the water. That splendid ceremony is vividly re-enacted by Venetians today, for their children and for tourists.

Except in the winter, much of the city's energy is devoted to tourism, the modern substitute for the riches once brought back to Venice by merchant and warrior fleets. Nowhere else has the practice of relieving visitors of their currency become such a refined art. But the city does offer a lot for the money!

The days when Venice was the invaluable merchant banker and the best bordello of Europe are long gone. Though a smattering of nobility with ducal-sounding names still remains, most of the wealthy people in Venice today are seasonal visitors. An extravagant ball on the Grand Canal is now the exception, not the rule.

Visitors find Venetians friendly, immensely fond of children in the Italian manner, professedly romantic, proud of being well-dressed, surprisingly superstitious, frequently self-infatuated and just a trifle patronizing toward anyone unlucky enough to have been born somewhere else. Their somewhat obscure dialect emphasizes the separateness of Venice. Unless lost, visitors are often amused to see the names of canals or districts spelled differently from one sign to another.

Venice, in flashes, is rounding a bend and coming upon a tiny stone bridge over a canal with a sleek black gondola tied

City without wheels: Venice's "street" levels rise two feet at high tide.

up below; it's feeding pigeons at Piazza San Marco, the unexpectedly frequent pleasure of the smell of coffee roasting, artists showing off their renditions of the city on the quays or at the cafés, honeymooners haggling sheepishly with a gondolier on the Grand Canal, a winter foghorn booming in from the Giudecca shipping canal, young boys kicking a football against a beautiful Renaissance church, plump tiger cats lining up in a *campo* to be fed fish bits and tomatoed spaghetti by an old woman, a laundry barge making its daily rounds with stacks of freshly ironed sheets for hotels, middle-aged couples holding hands in the world's most romantic moonlight, housewives choosing the best artichokes from a fruit-and-vegetable scow and the suggestive glimpse of an enormous, glittering chandelier through the ballroom window of a grandiose Gothic palace. **9**

A Brief History

As the setting for one of history's most fantastic and successful adventures, the Venetian lagoon hardly seems promising. But the remarkable fact is that a republic, built on stakes over this watery base and never comprising more than 200,000 citizens, managed to survive—and, indeed, flourish—for 1,100 years. During this time, Venice indelibly influenced the course of modern history. And left us an incomparable legacy—the city itself.

Fishermen and boatmen skilled at navigating among the shallow lagoon's silt and sand islands were the first Venetians. Despite local legend, these people did not just decide to found Venice one day in the 5th century A.D.; they were too busy fishing and extracting salt. The real instigation came from the Lombards, who invaded Italy in 568. This barbarian onslaught sent the coastal dwellers fleeing to the low-lying offshore islands in the lagoon, first to Torcello, then further out to Malamocco on the string of *lidi* exposed to the Adriatic.

Venetia, or Venezia, was the name of the entire area at the northern end of the Adriatic under the Roman empire. The beginning of present-day Venice developed very gradually around a cluster of small islands, including that of Rivo Alto, the future Rialto. The lagoon islands remained free of the Lombard kingdom and were only loosely controlled from the Roman-Byzantine centre at Ravenna.

In 697, the lagoon communities were united in a separate military command set up at Malamocco under a *dux* or doge. Though the first doges were probably selected by the lagoon dwellers themselves, they took their orders from the Byzantine emperor.

When the Franks succceeded the Lombards on the mainland in 774, Charlemagne sent his son Pépin to conquer the offshore upstart. He seized Malamocco, but not before the doge and his entourage were rowed over to Rivo Alto. There they settled until a fortress was built where the Doges' Palace now stands.

The Rise of the Republic

Gradually, Venice became independent of distant Byzantium, and it prospered—first from control of the northern Italian river deltas and then from the sea itself. Fishing, salt and lumber trade and the transport of slaves enriched the city. From the 9th century, Venice dared to traffic with the Moslems in defiance of both pope and Byzantine emperor. With Moslem gold and silver, the Venetians bought exotic Eastern luxuries from Constantinople, then sold them in Europe at great profit (a technique perfected over the centuries).

Although the obscure (probably Greek) St. Theodore was Venice's first patron saint, legend had always linked St. Mark the Evangelist with the northern Adriatic region. In 829, as local schoolchildren and most tourists learn today, two Venetian merchants went to Alexandria, Egypt, and stole the body of St. Mark, craftily concealing it under slabs of pork which they knew the Moslems wouldn't touch.

As soon as the precious relic reached Venice, construction of a chapel was begun next to the Doges' Palace: the original basilica of San Marco. Venice quickly adopted the evangelist and his winged lion as the city's symbol.

The newly founded Arsenal turned out fleets of stronger

The spoils of many republican forays enriched San Marco basilica.

and swifter galleys, enabling Venice to move deeper down into the Adriatic where she warred for decades with the powerful but less organized Dalmatian seafarers. The famous Doge Pietro Orseolo II, celebrating victory over the Dalmatian "pirates", started the annual "wedding the sea" ceremony in the year 1000 to denote Venice's supremacy over the Adriatic. Ships flying St. Mark's pennant, ranged over the Aegean and the eastern Mediterranean, trading and plundering, faithfully bringing spoils back to enrich the doges' treasury and strengthen the state. Venice **11**

came to be known as the Serenissima, queen of the seas.

From the start of the Crusades in 1095, the Venetians
sensed a bonanza. Little interested in the spiritual as-
pects, they eagerly produced
and outfitted ships, equipped
knights and often charged ex-
tortionate prices for the voyage to the holy places. Sometimes the religious warriors
were used to settle Venice's
commercial quarrels along the
way. The popes didn't ap-

prove, but it was good business—always top priority for
the republic. In the 12th century, the Venetians were as successful at piracy as the
Genoese, Greeks, Saracens,
Pisans, Sicilians and others
marauding around the Mediterranean.

A proud diplomatic
moment for Venice came in
1177 when Holy Roman Em-
peror Frederick I, known as
Barbarossa, made his peace
with Pope Alexander III by

Bellini's Processione in Piazza San Marco—*Venice 500 years ago.*

kneeling before him in the basilica of San Marco.

Much less proud was Venice's leading and cold-blooded role in the infamous Fourth Crusade, culminating in the seizure and sack of Constantinople in 1204. First, Doge Enrico Dandolo, almost blind and nearly 90 years old, charged the Crusaders vastly more than they had expected or could pay for equipment and transport. To earn their way, the knights were obliged to subdue some Dalmatian enemies for Venice, after which they were diverted to Constantinople, sacred capital of Christian civilization since the 4th century. There, the Crusaders staged bloody sieges, followed by murder, rape and pillage. One-quarter of the loot was given to a new emperor installed by Dandolo's forces in Constantinople; the Venetians and Crusaders divided up the rest. But to cover their debts, the hapless knights had to hand over most of their share to Venice.

As a result of this arrangement, Venice began calling itself "Lord and Master of a Quarter and a Half-Quarter of the Empire of Romania", or eastern Roman empire. The republic was now clearly a major power, controlling all the major points along the routes to Egypt and the Crimea. But the brutal saga of Constantinople made its name despised throughout much of the civilized world.

At the end of the 13th century, the Venetians curbed the powers of the doges by converting from a monarchy to **13** patrician oligarchy. The ruling Great Council was enlarged to over 1,000 noble members and the aristocracy cemented in power through a Council of Ten and other interlocking commissions.

Eventually, doges became little more than pampered prisoners in their magnificent palace, stripped of every vestige of authority, forbidden to take a holiday or contact the outside world without their counsellors' consent. From their election by a complicated procedure until their death, they were primarily there to preside over the republic's pompous festivities. (One doge, Marin Faliero, was even beheaded in 1355 for conspiring to assert some power; that was ruled an act of treason.) After 1310, no major change was made in the constitution until the republic fell in 1797.

Wars and Intrigue

For much of the 14th century, Venice battled on the high seas with her most dangerous rival, Genoa. The two great maritime powers, evenly matched in ships and ambition, competed bitterly everywhere: they fought over the slave and grain trade in the Black Sea and over the lucrative route out of the Mediterranean and north to Bruges or Antwerp. There spices and other Oriental wares could be traded for prized Flemish cloth, English wool and tin. Both nations transported salt from the small Balearic island of Ibiza and sweet Greek wines (which didn't "travel well" by wagon or pack animal) through the Straits of Gibraltar.

But Venice had overextended herself. Though she remained queen of the Adriatic, she was forced to cede Dalmatia to Hungary after 350 years of control, and during the 14th century the republic's power also declined on both Cyprus and Crete.

At home, it proved to be a turbulent century. In 1310, a group of disgruntled aristocrats under Baiamonte Tiepolo tried to seize power and kill the doge. The revolt was foiled (see p. 46). Then came the bubonic plague of 1347: almost half of Venice's population of 120,000 was wiped out in just 18 months by the Black Death. About 20,000 more Venetians died in another epidemic in 1382, and over the next three centuries, Venice was almost never free of plague, bubonic or pulmonary. At the Rialto, now a major European commercial banking centre, fortunes were made but more often lost as the republic bartered, badgered and borrowed to support its costly wars with Genoa.

In 1379, during the fourth and final Genoese war, Venice came closer to defeat than at any time in her history. The Genoese fleet captured and

In 1500 Venice reigned supreme as Europe's crossroads with the East.

sank Venetian ships in their home waters, while raiding parties burned settlements along the Lido. Manoeuvering in concert with Genoa, Hungarian and Paduan troops closed off Venice's mainland escape routes. When the key port of Chioggia, just south of Venice, was stormed and taken, the Serenissima seemed lost.

But the city rallied, blockaded the Lido lagoon entrance with ships chained together, sank barges laden with rocks in the channels to Chioggia, mounted cannons on galleys for the first time and hired the best available mercenaries to besiege Chioggia from the sand bars. Finally, in June 1380, the Genoese surrendered, leaving Venice exhausted but with its oligarchical institutions intact.

Recovery came quickly, reviving the old rapacious instincts. With no serious challenge to its maritime supremacy, the republic seized or bought many key ports in Greece and Albania and simultaneously moved deep into the Italian mainland—a portentous departure. Expanding as a manufacturing city in the 15th century, Venice needed food, wood and metal from the nearest possible

sources. But it could not expect to push along the northern Italian rivers and across the great plain of Lombardy without meeting opposition. Its professional forces, led by a series of mercenary captains or *condottieri* (they worked by contract, *condotta*), inevitably provoked the powerful Visconti duchy of Milan. A series of conflicts, called the Lombard wars, began in 1425. The republic defended its new territory so tenaciously that Milan, Florence and Naples formed an anti-Venice coalition. Europe worried about Venice taking over the entire Italian peninsula.

The New Rival

However, a new and vastly menacing rival arose in the East against Venice: the Ottoman empire. The war preparations of Mohammed the Conqueror, the new, 19-year-old sultan, were not taken seriously, and the Turks captured Constantinople in 1453. In the following years, they harassed Venetian trade routes and finally won a key naval battle at Negroponte in the north Aegean in 1470. Though the Serenissima was still the leading Mediterranean maritime power, stronger than any single force on the Italian mainland, these defeats by the Turks marked the beginning of a long downhill slide. In the wake of Constantinople, the Venetian senate came up with the idea of taxing its citizens. Of Venice's many innovations, this is undoubtedly the least popular.

While its fortunes beyond the lagoon waned, Venice became the centre of a magnificent cultural outpouring and the magnet for increasing

Guardi's painting of the Bucintoro underscores Venice's maritime role. **17**

numbers of visitors. There was no more sumptuous building anywhere than the Doges' Palace, no church filled with as many exotic treasures—and so architecturally eccentric—as San Marco. Artists like the Bellinis, Giorgione, Carpaccio, Titian, Veronese and Tintoretto made Venetian painting the most enduring of the republic's glories. The revolutionary concepts of Andrea Palladio shaped the future of architecture; the republic's lawyers, physicians, book printers, mathematicians and Greek scholars were renowned throughout Europe. And, for much of the Western world's élite, there was nothing quite so chic as a palace copied after one of those disparate masterpieces along the Grand Canal.

In 1498 Vasco da Gama of Portugal undertook his epic voyage around Africa's Cape of Good Hope to India, putting an end to the Venetian spice-trade monopoly. During the same period of prodigious exploration, Christopher Columbus's landfalls on the other side of the Atlantic signalled something equally momentous for the republic: Europe gradually turned towards the Western hemisphere, losing interest in that oriental trade which had ensured Venetian prosperity for so long.

After surrendering vital Greek and Albanian ports to the Turks in 1503, Venice found herself six years later facing almost all of Europe, allied in the League of Cambrai under Pope Julius II. This unlikely coalition claimed to be preparing a new crusade against the Turks. In fact, it was aimed primarily at Venice's empire, which stretched across most of northern Italy.

First, the pope excommunicated Venice. Like many other Vatican decrees though, this was largely ignored. Next, city after city defected as the republic's 20,000-man mercenary army fell apart. For a while, things seemed truly desperate. But once again the Venetians prevailed. They recaptured strategic Padua, and after the pope and the Spanish King Charles I (Holy Roman Emperor Charles V) changed sides in an effort to drive the French from Italy, Venice managed to regain most of her ravaged territory. Though inconclusive in the end, the seven-year war did quash the Serenissima's ambitions in Italy. Thereafter, with Charles V's empire steadily ac-

VENETIAN REPUBLIC
IN THE MID-16TH CENTURY

cumulating Italian territory, all of Venice's diplomatic skill was needed to preserve her own independence.

And, around the Mediterranean the Ottomans surged on: they conquered Syria and Egypt in 1517, Rhodes in 1522, and with the Barbary pirates took Algiers in 1529. From Albania all the way round to Morocco, the coast became Turkish. For Christian Europe, it was a serious menace.

In 1571, the Venetian fleet joined units sent by Spain and the pope, and defeated the Turks in the monumental naval battle of Lepanto. The Holy League of Christians, Venetians included, lost some 9,000 men at Lepanto, the Turks 30,000. Unfortunately, the impressive performance of

the galleys of St. Mark in this battle was overshadowed by a strategic loss. After a fierce struggle, the Turks took over Venice's stronghold on Cyprus—a devastating blow for the Serenissima's eastern Mediterranean commerce.

About 60,000 people, roughly one-third of the republic's population, perished in severe epidemics of the plague between 1575 and 1577. Fifty years later, barely recovered, Venice was struck by its last major outbreak of the Black Death: the populace shrank from 150,000 to only 100,000.

Paradoxically, in spite of plague, famine and a diminished empire, Venice continued to prosper in the 16th and 17th centuries. The Venetians began manufacturing **19**

In Venice, as elsewhere in Italy, cats top the urban fauna league.

a foreign army. Its treasures were not ravaged, and artists of all descriptions continued to create new ones. With Claudio Monteverdi in the 17th century and Antonio Vivaldi in the 18th, Venice produced more operas and had more opera houses than any other European city. In fact, Venice's public opera house, which opened in 1637, was the first of its kind anywhere. Tiepolo and Canaletto painted Venice for the world. Carlo Goldoni's new adaptations of *commedia dell'arte* broke exciting theatrical ground. Venetian girls' choirs, stage-set designers, organists and organ builders were the toast of the continent.

If Venice was fading from the world power stage after centuries of pre-eminence, it didn't seem to matter. Europe had never seen such wild carnival balls, such comely courtesans, such extravagant gambling.

Those two famous coffee houses which still grace Piazza San Marco opened in the 18th century, quickly becoming the fashionable meeting spots for the idle rich of Venice and the grandest of the Grand Tourists. Everybody who was anybody owned at least one gondola complete with singing

woollen cloth with striking success, their glassware and printed books found expanding markets, some spice commerce came back to the Mediterranean, Jewish refugees brought desirable skills and trading contacts to Venice, and the city's political stability appealed to traders and commercial investors.

And, always, the pilgrims and tourists came. Unlike many other European cities, Venice was never occupied by

gondolier. It was impossibly amusing (and, of course, very good business for local merchants). Hardly anybody noticed the republic's last naval adventures—skirmishes with Barbary pirates off the North African coast.

But everybody—the doge, the Council of Three state inquisitors with their secret-police network, the once feared Council of Ten and all the other commissions of nobles in Venice's oligarchy—noticed the forces of Napoleon Bonaparte swarming across northern Italy from Milan. Too quickly, the French were at the lagoon's doorstep.

The End of the Republic

Most ordinary Venetians remained loyal, as they always had, unimpressed by the strange "democratic" slogans of the 1789 Revolution or by Bonapartist agents plotting coups in back-canal palaces. But the city was effectively defenceless, its troops out of practice. There hadn't been a proper war for 80 years.

Seizing the lavish mainland estates of the highest Venetian aristocracy, Napoleon thundered that he would be the "Attila" of the lagoon city. He demanded that the government turn its power over to a democratic council under French military protection.

At the final meeting of the Great Council, on May 12, 1797, the last doge, Ludovico Manin, abdicated in tears. The council voted to dissolve itself, and the Serenissima passed into history.

Although Venice had never been particularly beloved in the Western world, her demise touched off many nostalgic obituaries. William Wordsworth's "On the Extinction of the Venetian Republic" contained these famous lines:

Once did she hold the gorgeous East in fee;
And was the safeguard of the West;
The worth of Venice did not fall below her birth,
Venice, the eldest child of Liberty.

Untroubled by nostalgia, Napoleon let his 4,000 soldiers loot Venice methodically that summer. From the basilica of San Marco and the Doges' Palace, the mint, the Arsenal, the archives, the fleet, the galleries and the great palaces, almost no treasures escaped, not even the doge's ceremonial galley, the *Bucintoro,* which was burned. **21**

In October, Napoleon signed a treaty transferring Venice to Austrian control. Eight years later, after defeating Austria at Austerlitz, he reoccupied the city, making it part of his short-lived Kingdom of Italy. After Waterloo, the Austrians again occupied Venice (1815–66). They—like the French—were despised by the citizenry, but at least the Austrians did restore to the city most of Napoleon's artistic booty. They also linked Venice to the mainland for the first time, in 1846, by erecting an unsightly railway bridge.

Catching Europe's contagious revolutionary fever in 1848, the Venetians under Daniele Manin (unrelated to the last doge) rose up and ousted the Austrian garrison. They declared an independent "republic", which hung on through bombardment, blockade and cholera for 17 months. When the Austrian commander, Marshal Radetzky, arrived at Piazza San Marco in triumph, not one Venetian showed up. Happily, though thousands of shells were fired during this heroic but futile rebellion, Venice's great art treasures were not damaged.

In 1866, after Austria's defeat by Prussia, the Vene-tians voted overwhelmingly in a plebiscite to join the new Kingdom of Italy. Venice eventually became the capital of one of the peninsula's 20 regions, an insignificant role for a former world power, but all that the city could ever expect from Rome.

Nothing of great consequence occurred in Venice until 1902 when the Campanile of San Marco collapsed (see p. 44); some citizens still consider this the major event of

Undiminished by the years, the splendour of Piazza San Marco.

the 20th century. Venice survived both world wars without major damage. The Italians staged operations against the Austrians from Venice in World War I; the Germans occupied it for a period in World War II. New Zealand and British troops liberated the city in 1945, their officers moving immediately into the Danieli and other famous hotels. In a postwar referendum, the Venetians and other Italians voted to abolish the monarchy and become a republic.

Venice has earned world sympathy in its struggle against the traditional danger from water and the newer menace of pollution. But, as always, Venice continues to prosper from its mainstays—shipping and tourism. **23**

What to See

Venice is a maze of waterways and walkways. Though confusing at first, after a day or two it's surprisingly easy to get your bearings in what turns out to be a small, logically arranged city.

Immensely helpful yellow markers are posted everywhere, pointing the way to San Marco (St. Mark's), Rialto or Accademia. Obviously, it's wise to fix these three major landmarks in your mind right away.

The Venetian public-transport system is an absolute delight. Thanks to a government subsidy, the fares are low, and you'll find that the *vaporetti* (waterbuses) along the Grand Canal pass very frequently. Though they may be crowded during Venice's rush hours, the fabulous scenery to port and starboard should compensate.

Two *vaporetti,* Nos. 1 and 5, deserve special mention. The first runs from the central car park *(Piazzale Roma)* and the railway station *(Ferrovia)*, along the Grand Canal, past St. Mark's Basin and on to the Lido, stopping at just about every station. The trip, which takes perhaps an hour in either direction, is an excellent way to orientate yourself on your first day in Venice. Faster services run directly to Piazza San Marco from either end of the line.

No. 5 should be everybody's favourite. Called the *circolare,* it actually makes two half-circles around Venice, taking in several of the closest islands. It is the only *vaporetto* to chug along the canal through the famous Arsenal—your chance for a glimpse of that famous shipyard (see p. 71).

First Impressions

Venice, like Florence, has far too many works of art to absorb in a brief span of time. For many visitors, all that culture tends to become somewhat overwhelming. It's good advice to mix up your sightseeing, taking a boat ride between churches, a stroll between galleries, spending the odd hour at an outdoor café.

Of course, for much of the year, the heat serves as a brake on over-exertion; tourists are forced to emulate the Venetians and take things very casually. It's ever so much better that way: this is a city to be savoured like a rare cognac, not gulped.

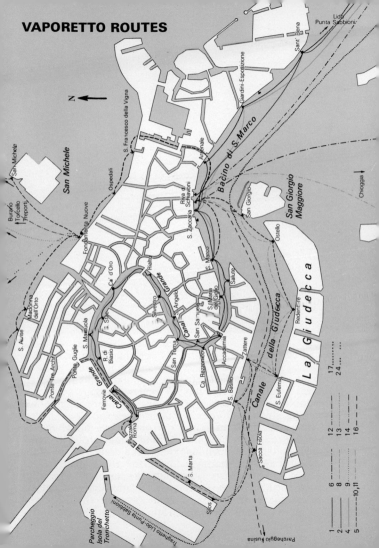

VAPORETTO ROUTES

Canal Grande
(Grand Canal)

Difficult as it is for a visitor to get used to the idea, this unforgettable waterway serves as the main street of Venice. Sweeping majestically in an inverted *S* through the city, the Grand Canal is so compellingly beautiful and fascinatingly busy that many tourists ride back and forth on the *vaporetti* for hours, taking it all in.

For more leisurely viewing, nothing beats a gondola. Though hardly an inexpensive adventure, it should prove to be memorable and instructive; Venetian gondoliers are gold mines of information about their *canalazzo*.

Roughly two miles long, the Grand Canal probably originated as a branch of one of the mainland rivers then flowing into the lagoon. Along its banks stand some 200 palaces built between the 12th and 18th centuries—Byzantine

No motors or waves in bygone days, and swimmers had the right) way.

...nd Gothic, Lombard and Baroque, some carefully restored, others sadly crumbling, few still inhabited by the grandly aristocratic families for whom they were constructed. Today they house municipal offices, hotels, museums and even, during the winter, Venice's casino.

Façades along this amazing palatial parade, notably the gilded Ca' d'Oro, have been imitated all over the world, in Leningrad as well as New York. Quite simply, no main street even remotely resembles the Grand Canal. It's hardly surprising that millions of visitors have fallen in love with Venice during their first trip along the famous waterway.

Lord Byron swam in the Grand Canal; Wagner worked on *Tristan and Isolde* in one of its palaces; Henry James, A.E. Housman, Ruskin, Robert Browning, Goethe, Hemingway, Mark Twain, Winston Churchill, kings, queens, popes, emperors and presidents stayed here; doges died here for centuries, painters have painted it, honeymooners have been poled along it, Europe's grandest balls have taken place here.

Pleasant embankments line the Grand Canal at the Rialto Bridge—one of the few places where you can actually stroll along beside the famous waterway. Until the last century, this was the only bridge spanning the canal. Now, two more bridges and a handful of ferries *(traghetti)* enable you to get from one side to the other.

Up and down the Grand Canal about 20,000 Venetians **27**

commute daily by waterbus. Many live in the modern industrial suburbs on the mainland. Gondolas, water taxis, *sandoli* (small, two-oared skiffs), the *vaporetti,* and similar municipal *motoscafi,* garbage barges, red-grey post-office speed-boats, fruit and vegetable boats, black-and-gold funeral launches, police inboards, eel-fishermen's outboards, cement scows and rowing skiffs move along this boulevard, in and out of the 45 canals which run into it, practically never colliding—although there's only one traffic light in town.

Of Gondolas and Gondoliers

Nothing is more quintessentially Venetian than the gondola, that elegant, slender queen of the canals. More than 400 years ago, the Venetian senate decreed that all gondolas, except those used in regattas, must be painted black. Until the last century, there were some 10,000 gondolas in Venice; the wealthiest

Ever proudly proficient, gondoliers perpetuate a waning tradition.

aristocratic families might have had five or six tied up to colourful poles in front of their palaces.

Before the big bridges were built, the gondola was an indispensable urban and cross-lagoon mode of transport. Today, sadly, there are fewer than 500 of the beloved craft left in Venice. Nowadays, gondola-travel is limited almost exclusively to tourists.

The cross-canal ferry gondolas, on the other hand, are still a going concern. These workhorses of the fleet may be somewhat larger than the ordinary variety. You'll notice Venetian commuters casually standing up even when these gondolas bob in high waves; they're so ingeniously constructed that it's practically impossible to capsize them. The fare for the cross-canal trip goes on the gondola bench, not into the hand of the gondolier.

The word gondola may come from the Latin *cymbula* (small boat) or the Greek *kondi* (conch, seashell): scholars argue, no one is certain. Boats plying among the lagoon islands were called gondolas at least as early at the 11th century, though the graceful, elongated version so familiar today didn't take shape until

sometime in the 15th century.

Modern gondolas weigh about 1,300 pounds and are constructed by hand of 280 separate pieces of wood. The lopsided shape is necessary to counter-balance the weight of the gondolier on the poop. By tradition, the unusual oar-rest the gondolier uses only occasionally is carved out of a solid block of walnut.

Today Venice has only 470 gondoliers. Four centuries ago there were 20,000. Apprentice gondoliers take three years to learn to pilot the craft with acceptable expertise, fathers often passing their skill on to their sons. With their straw **29** hats and sailor's jumpers or striped T-shirts, the gondoliers still exhibit the caustic wit for which they're noted. Yet very few will sing anymore, preferring to follow along behind a barge equipped for the tourists with a professional serenader.

About 50 gondoliers pole the cross-canal ferries. For some years, they've threatened to stop that important municipal service because of the increasing motorboat traffic. Theoretically, the speed limit on canals is five kilometres per hour, eight in the lagoon near inhabited areas, no limit in open water. The gondolas, battered by the splashing of powerboats, must often be taken in for repairs and scraping. They are, however, far stronger than they look.

A trip to Venice may be something of an extravagance; a gondola ride along the canals—the ultimate Venetian experience—is unquestionably one. You may hear that gondola rates are municipally fixed; in practice, some visitors "successfully" bargain the price down slightly, but never to an inexpensive level. Be that as it may, there's nothing quite like the magic of a silent gondola glide through Venice's canals.

Ponte di Rialto
(Rialto Bridge)
Venice without the Rialto Bridge? Unthinkable. This familiar landmark, lined with a double row of shops, has proudly spanned the Grand Canal since Antonio da Ponte erected it nearly 400 years ago. Until late in the 12th century, there was no bridge at all over the great waterway; then pontoon-lighters were put across here, followed by several wooden bridges which either collapsed, wore out or were sabotaged.

A famous Carpaccio painting in the Accademia shows the last of the wooden spans, a decrepit drawbridge affair. Michelangelo was among the many who submitted plans for a replacement, but da Ponte's bold design carried the day. His bridge has proved structurally powerful if visually controversial.

Rialto, derived from Rivo Alto (high bank), was settled by the first Venetians in the 9th century. Ever since, this district, covering both sides of the Grand Canal, has been the city's commercial hub. During the peak of the republic's influence, it was as important as any financial centre in Europe. Less grandly, the quarter was also famous for its brothels.

Today, minus most of the banks and all of the bordellos, this is the busiest shopping area in Venice. On the Rialto Bridge, there are jewelry, clothing, shoe, perfume and souvenir shops, along with hordes of hawkers selling all kinds of trinkets. Guides nowadays warn tourists on the bridge not to "spit on the gondolas"; in the good old days, the cry was "don't spit on the swimmers".

The bridge leads directly down into the liveliest section of Venice, the **outdoor markets**—the *erheria* and *pescheria*. Venetian housewives, chefs and servants have been

Tables near historic bridge are scarce but worth waiting for.

buying their fruit, vegetables, fish and meat at the stalls here since 1097. The marvellously colourful, noisy spectacle, free for the viewing every morning except Sundays and holidays, is Venice at its bustling, natural best.

Depending on the season, the vendors will be singing out the praises of melons, peaches, artichokes, red Treviso lettuce, grapes, mushrooms, oranges, strawberries. Some **31** stands specialize only in cheese, and here you can really "get it wholesale"—if you're willing to buy one of those giant five- or ten-kilogram drums of *parmigiano* (parmesan), or *provolone*.

The *erberia* merges gradually into what must be the best fish market in Europe. Set mostly among the columns of an ancient portico. Venice's *pescheria* features fish at its absolute freshest. It's a rare day when you won't see huge sea turtles flat on their crusty shells, waving their prehistoric-looking flippers at prospective buyers. Eels and crabs, scampi and octopus, mussels and sea bass are invitingly displayed, jovial fishmongers with chapped hands and hip boots hack away at giant tunny (tuna), and alley cats make swift passes at sardines.

While there are a few mini-supermarkets in Venice and scores of small grocery and butchers' shops, the vast majority of people prefer the Rialto markets. It's universally assumed that the goods are freshest and the prices cheapest at the Rialto—or at least there's the hope of haggling.

Venice's fish market offers wide selection of Adriatic varieties.

San Marco Area

Piazza San Marco
(St. Mark's Square)
Venetians call it simply the *Piazza,* since it's always been the only square in the city deemed worthy of the name. Napoleon called it the "drawing room of Europe"* and countless other visitors have lavished every conceivable

---
* Other sources have him praising it as "the most beautiful drawing room in the world" or "the drawing room of Venice".

SAN MARCO

superlative on this breathtaking space.

The Piazza is in fact a trapezoid, its proportions irregular, its uneven pavement sloping slightly downwards towards the basilica. The trachyte (volcanic rock) paving strips, 250 years old, lie over five or six earlier layers of tile dating back to the mid-13th century, when the garden of a nearby monastery was turned into a piazza.

Down through the centuries, the Piazza was always the political and religious centre of Venice. Splendid processions, unrivalled anywhere, were staged here; one is brilliantly illustrated in Gentile Bellini's famous painting at the Accademia (see p. 56). Victorious commanders returning home from the Genoese or Turkish wars were honoured at lavish ceremonies in front of the basilica, while vendors sold sweets and snacks to the crowds just as they do today.

In the Piazza's arcades, European knights and clergymen setting out on crusades would buy souvenirs and provisions for their voyage.

The three reddish-brown flagpoles in front of San Marco have been there since 1505. Now they fly the banners of Italy side by side with those of Venice.

From the clock tower runs the 500-year-old **Procuratie Vecchie,** now an office building but originally the dazzling residence of the procurators, nine Venetians of considerable influence charged with the administration of San Marco. Across the Piazza is the **Procu-** 33

ratie Nuove, built about 100 years later, at present a museum. Linking the two of them is "Napoleon's wing" *(Ala Napoleonica),* another museum (see p. 66), previously an Italian royal palace. The wing replaced the San Geminiano church which Napoleon ordered torn down. (Napoleon's architectural hatchetwork won him few friends in Venice. They never got around to placing his statue in the central niche reserved for it here among the Roman emperors.)

For much of the 19th century, Venice lived under hated Austrian domination. In the Piazza, the emotions of the occupation were played out daily: since the Austrians took their coffee at Quadri's café, the Venetians patronized only Florian's. The Venetians stolidly ignored Austrian parades and band concerts in the Piazza, forbidding their children to applaud.

Nowadays children are rarely restrained in the huge square. Aside from feeding the pigeons, their favourite pastime is straddling the two marble lions which, since 1722,

have gazed out from the Piazzetta dei Leoncini to the left of the basilica. For parents, this is one of Venice's compulsory photographs, and if you lack a camera, there'll always be someone on hand to take a snapshot for delivery to your hotel. In the solid building behind the lions lived two of Venice's religious heroes, Pius X and John XXIII, in their pre-papal days.

As pictures and paintings all over the city remind you, the Piazza is often flooded. By far the worst inundation of modern times is commemorated by a small marble slab at the base of the Campanile, marking the water level—about waist high—on November 4, 1966. Although some people found it amusing to paddle about the Piazza in boats or go to the cafés by gondola, this exceptionally high flood demonstrated how vulnerable Venice, with all her treasures, remains.

But under water, covered with snow, glistening in sunlight, any way at any time, the Piazza is beautiful. It is no less awesome with a handful of late-night strollers than with 40,000 people jammed within the arcades on a summer Sunday morning. This is where the action is, and what a setting!

Throngs stroll where doges honoured their victorious commanders.

35

Pampered Pigeons

It's believed there are twice as many pigeons as people living in Venice—some 200,000 of the grey-blue or occasionally all-white birds so beloved by children and deplored by conservationists. Since they first appeared here, pigeons have been officially protected, for reasons which remain obscure. One legend has it that a flock of pigeons carrying crosses led Venice's founders to the original site. More authoritative sources agree that pigeons didn't turn up before the 12th century. They've often been called symbols of Venice's serenity, a play on Serenissima.

For decades the birds were formally fed twice a day at their favourite pecking point, the Piazza. That custom stopped several years ago with "Operation Pigeon", a quickly abandoned scheme to reduce the winged population—and its damages—by netting, the Pill and restricting seed distribution to historically unimportant parts of the city. Bird-lovers won the day over art lovers who claimed that pigeons were abetting the decay of Venice's priceless statuary and menacing public health.

A veritable industry thrives on the pigeons, particularly around the Piazza: vendors sell a small quantity of corn or other seed wrapped in newspaper for an outrageous price, freelance photographers are eager to snap your children with pigeons perched on their heads and you may even be "offered" a learned discourse, by the odd conman, on the role of pigeons in Venetian history. Economy note: take along your own bread or rolls; pigeons aren't all that fussy.

Basilica di San Marco
(St. Mark's Basilica)

Mysteriously Eastern, gloriously Western, Venice's renowned cathedral is one of the most incredible buildings the world has ever seen. Somehow, San Marco manages to convey utterly harmonious beauty, despite the fact that it encompasses a mixture of styles and irregular construction. Each of its five low domes, for example, has different proportions. Its façade is a conglomeration of widely varying styles and periods and very few of its 500 columns match.

The church was first built in 830 to house the body of St. Mark (stolen from Alexandria by two Venetian adventurers) and as a chapel for the doges who lived next door. With St. Mark as Venice's patron saint, the basilica became the republic's shrine. Doges were crowned at its altar and buried in its crypts. In 976, the original, largely wooden, church burned down in a terrible fire. It was rebuilt, then dismantled, and the basilica we know went up between 1063 and 1094.

Glittering mosaics crown entrance to the 900-year-old basilica.

One of those legends so loved by Venetians recounts the miraculous history of St. Mark's body. The city, clearly, would not want to be without the relics of its patron, particularly when other cities might claim him as their saint. According to the story, St. Mark's body was so well and safely hidden within the church that it survived the blaze of 976. But nobody could find it. Then, it's said, during the consecration of the new church on June 25, 1094, one arm soon followed by the rest of the "lost" body appeared from within a pillar to the right of the main altar—the answer to the city's prayers. Once again the body was carefully secreted, the tale continues, and gradually over the centuries the location was *again* forgotten. But during repairs to the basilica in 1811, St. Mark's body was supposedly found once more and placed under the high altar where it's solemnly revered today.

As guides and Venetians shamelessly inform visitors, not only was St. Mark's body "stolen" from the East, but so was almost everything else in the basilica. Many of the church's columns, far older than Venice itself, were brought back as booty from republican forays in the Levant, like so many of its religious treasures.

The basilica is open daily from early morning until at least nightfall, with sightseeing firmly discouraged during mass. San Marco is at its most spectacular during Easter services.

The upper level, Pala d'Oro and treasury may be visited for limited periods in the morning and afternoon (see p. 113).

Inside or out, San Marco conveys a captivating, exotic atmosphere.

As in most other Italian churches, respectable dress is required of anyone entering San Marco. Visitors in shorts, bare-backed dresses and so on are turned away, though women no longer need to cover their heads with scarves.

The origin of San Marco's famous **horses** remains a mystery. After years of exhaustive study, all the specialists can say for sure is that the horses were cast in Greece or Rome between 400 B.C. and A.D. 200. The only ancient *quadriga* (four horses abreast) around today, they must be the world's best-travelled equine team.

Once they crowned Trajan's Arch in Rome; then they were moved to the imperial hippodrome in Constantinople. Doge Dandolo claimed them as victory spoils in 1204 and brought them to Venice. After guarding the Arsenal shipyard for a while, the horses were set up on San Marco, becoming a celebrated symbol of the Serenissima.

Napoleon had them taken to Paris, where they stood for 13 years in the Place du Carrousel. The Austrians charitably restored them to San Marco. They remained there until World War I, when the Italian government moved them to Rome. During World War II, the Venetians hid the horses in the nearby countryside. They will, vows Venice, never be allowed to leave again.

It now turns out that the horses are less bronze than assumed: they're mostly copper, covered with a gold-leaf crust scratched in precise arcs by Byzantine artisans to make their golden gilding glitter in the sunlight. But because recent testing showed that the

The original horses have been moved inside San Marco, where you'll also see fine Noah mosaic.

horses were suffering from atmospheric pollution, they have been moved inside the basilica where they can be seen at close range. Copies are being made to replace the originals on the balcony outside.

To the right of the basilica's main entrance, 42 steep steps lead to a small museum—featuring a 200-year old bass instrument, mosaics, tapestries, ancient artefacts and an amazing winged lion of wood—and to the balcony, with its fine pigeon's-eye view of the piazza.

Afterwards, you may stroll inside along narrow catwalks through the entire upper part of the basilica. Here the **mosaics** on the stunningly decorated upper walls are almost within reach. You'll notice some of the mosaic figures wearing red socks or footwear, a sign of membership in the noble House of David. Conveniently placed on this upper level are several coin-operated machines to explain everything you see in English, French, German, Italian or Spanish.

The magical interior of San Marco is covered with about one acre of mosaics, the earliest dating back more than 800 years. Among the most beautiful are some from the 13th century depicting Old Testament events on the ceiling of the church's narthex. On the marble floor in front of the main doorway here, a reddish stone marks the spot where the doge forced a reconciliation between Pope Alexander III and Barbarossa in 1177.

Only with patience and a sharp eye will you count all the Pala's gems.

Although Byzantine, the shimmering backdrop to the basilica's high altar is one of Christendom's richest treasures. Begun 1,000 years ago in Constantinople, the **Pala d'Oro** was embellished and enlarged several times on doges' orders until it arrived at its present form in 1342. Napoleon removed some of the screen's jewels, but there are still a total of 2,486: 1,300 pearls, 400 garnets, 300 sapphires, 300 emeralds, 90 amethysts, 75 balas-rubies, 15 rubies, 4 topazes and 2 cameos. Almost everything else is gold, exquisitely wrought.

The Pala revolves, so that during solemn high mass its jewelled representation of Christ imparting his blessing, surrounded by glittering angels, apostles and prophets, faces the main altar and congregation beyond.

To see the Pala d'Oro, visitors pay a small sum that also enables them to visit the **treasury** *(tesoro)* off the baptistery on the basilica's right side. Here, in two small vaulted chambers, are displayed exasperatingly anonymous but obviously ancient relics, including some bones and skulls, onyx pieces, chalices and incense censers, icons and medallions, candelabra and delicate glassware. It's believed that Marco Polo brought some of these items back from China.

The atmosphere in this small, musty place is hushed, and a prominent sign printed in five languages requests respect and reverence. Unfortunately, as custodians like to point out, the treasury today contains only a fraction of the precious Eastern booty it held during Venice's heyday. Napoleon is blamed for having removed some of the gold and silver and a number of the treasury's diamonds for Josephine's crown.

Campanile di San Marco
(St. Mark's Bell Tower)

Towering over San Marco and the entire city is this bell tower to top all bell towers. The Campanile is to Venetians what Big Ben is to Londoners. Incredible as it may seem, the original bell tower stood for almost 1,000 years; it was enlarged over the centuries to its maximum height of 324 feet.

Watch-tower, signal beacon, weathervane, gun turret and belfry, the Campanile served its republic proudly—and unfalteringly. Its bells rang out over the whole lagoon to greet victorious armadas returning from faraway seas. Up its spiral ramp on horseback rode dignitaries like Emperor Frederick III. And when Goethe came to Venice 200 years ago, he supposedly climbed to the top for his first view of the sea. A grim medieval custom was to dangle violators of church laws from the belfry in wooden cages. Suicide plunges were not uncommon in later times. Galileo is said to have taken a

For the priceless view on high it's worth taking the expensive lift ride.

doge to the top of the Campanile to show off his new telescope.

Just before 10 a.m. on July 14, 1902, the grand old tower collapsed gracefully into the Piazza below, an event Venetians still discuss in detail and with theatrical despair, as if the calamity occurred only last month. In gentlemanly fashion, they say, the Campanile had "warned" of its impending demise by creaking and developing some cracks. So, the area was roped off and when the end came, no one was hurt. An early photographer took a memorable shot of the falling tower.

Viewed from atop the Campanile, St. Mark's basin is endlessly busy.

The city council quickly decided to rebuild the Campanile "as it was, where it was" *(com'era, dov'era),* a phrase now part of Venetian lore. Exactly 1,000 years after the erection of the original Campanile, on April 25, 1912, the nearly precise replica which stands today was inaugurated, delighting Venice lovers worldwide, many of whom had contributed funds for the project.

The new version, many hundreds of tons lighter than the original, is believed to be sound enough to last another millenium. Jacopo Sansovino's beautiful 16th-century *loggetta,* recently restored by the British Venice in Peril Fund, serves as the Campanile's entrance.

The ride up in the new lift (elevator) lasts scarcely a minute. On a clear day, the view—of the Adriatic, the *lidi* sheltering Venice, the lagoon islands, the mainland shores and snow-topped Alps to the north—is justly celebrated. Strangely, from on high, the city itself seems to have no canals, but its compact nature is evident.

For an even better view of the city, the best outside of an aeroplane, go to the top of the *campanile* on little San Giorgio island a few hundred yards out in St. Mark's basin (see p. 52).

Torre dell'Orologio
(Clock Tower)

Speaking of towers, consider that marvellously colourful example across the Piazza from the Campanile. For almost 500 years, the two famous **Moors** atop the clock tower have been hammering the hours on their great bell, delighting crowds below. Somehow, they've dented the bell only slightly, as you'll see when you climb the 136 winding steps up to this beloved Venetian landmark.

The muscular, green-bronze Moors, somewhat scantily dressed, lift their mallets to strike each hour as soon as a small signal bell rings across the way on the basilica of San Marco.

Tourists are sometimes ad-

Take your camera to film Moor's swinging hourly performance.

vised to stay off the tower when the Moors are hammering, but in fact the noise is not particularly deafening. Venetians claim that last century a workman was hit by a Moor's mallet and knocked into the square below. Keep the children in hand! Another durable Venetian belief: anyone stroking the Moors' exposed nether regions is assured of sexual potency for a year.

The clock tower itself features the inevitable winged lion and a splendid zodiacal clock which shows the time in Arabic and Roman numerals. During Ascension week in May, three bright-eyed Magi and a trumpeting angel swing out of the face of the tower every hour and, stiffly bowing, rotate around a gilded madonna. Like everything on the tower, this spectacle dates back to the end of the 15th century.

Through the clock tower's archway, on the left side of the smart shopping street, the Merceria, look for a stone relief of a woman. It commemorates one of Venice's favourite legends: the "old lady of the mortar" who leaned out of her window in 1310 to find out what all the noise was about and saw Baiamonte Tiepolo's revolutionary forces heading into the Piazza to battle the doge's army. She accidentally knocked a stone mortar on to the head of Tiepolo's flag bearer, felling him and sending the rebels back to the Rialto in confusion. The threat was over and the old lady became a heroine of the republic (see p. 14).

Clock tells time three different ways and shows phases of moon.

Piazzetta di San Marco

If Napoleon thought the Piazza was Venice's drawing room, then, Venetians say, the Piazzetta must be its vestibule. Those two soaring **columns** of granite greeting anyone arriving at St. Mark's basin by sea were booty from Constantinople or Syria. Laboriously hoisted upright in 1172, they haven't budged since: a third pillar fell into the water during the unloading and has never been recovered.

On top of one column is a figure with his back to the sea, popularly supposed to be St. Theodore, Venice's original patron saint. On the other stands the winged lion of St. Mark, damaged during a Paris sojourn arranged by Napoleon.

According to one of Venice's oldest superstitions, walking between the Piazzetta's two columns meant certain death. In former times, it seems, enemies of the republic were executed here. But most Venetians, not to mention hundreds of thousands of tourists, blithely ignore the legend and pass between these monumental gateway pillars to the city.

On one side of the Piazzetta stands Jacopo Sansovino's 16th-century masterpiece, the lavish **Libreria Vecchia** with wonderful columns and sculptures. The great architect, a Florentine who fled Rome in 1527, supposedly had to clear shops, eating places and wooden public toilets out of the Piazzetta before starting his library and *loggetta* at the Campanile's base.

Most young visitors find Venice's pigeon problem no problem at all!

About 1,000 years ago, the Piazzetta was a boat basin and water reached the great Piazza. When *acqua alta* spills over the quay, flooding the regal "vestibule", it's easy to visualize the original arrangement.

Palazzo Ducale
(Doges' Palace)

For about nine centuries, this appropriately magnificent palace was the seat of the republic and residence of most of Venice's doges. It remains almost exactly as it was 400 years ago, rich with reminders of the many great moments of history that have taken place here.

First built in fortress-like Byzantine style in the 9th century, the palace was partially replaced 500 years later by a Gothic structure. (The two windows on the lagoon side which are set lower indicate the 14th-century construction.) Three devastating fires necessitated extensive reconstruction: the result is a unique combination of Byzantine, Gothic and Renaissance.

The palace's astounding 15th-century entranceway is called the **Porta della Carta** (Paper Gate), because the

doge's decrees were nailed to it. Just to the left are the mysterious **Tetrarchs,** known as the Four Moors. Some experts assert that the embracing redstone figures represent Diocletian and associates; others say they're four Saracen robbers who tried to loot the basilica's treasury through the wall behind them. Sculpted in the

In the grandest palace of them all 120 doges presided over Venice.

4th century, this curious ensemble came to Venice 900 years later from Acre (in present-day Israel).

In front of them, at the corner of the basilica, is another bit of 13th-century booty from Acre: a pillar stump known as the **Pietra del Bando.** Here, the republic's new laws were proclaimed and, during the republic's more gruesome periods, traitors' heads were displayed to encourage good civic behaviour.

49

Inside the courtyard is the impressive **Scala dei Giganti**, a stairway named after Sansovino's colossal statues of Neptune and Mars, symbolizing Venice's land and sea power. Tourists normally use the only slightly less glamorous **Scala d'Oro.**

Upstairs, you'll see the luxurious apartments where the doges lived and the beautifully decorated rooms where the Serenissima's business was conducted. In the **Anti-Colle-**

Golden stairway, gigantic chamber bedazzle visitors to ducal palace.

gio, art lovers cluster in front of Paolo Veronese's *Rape of Europa* and Jacopo Tintoretto's *Bacchus and Ariadne*. Other notable works by Veronese adorn the meeting room of the Council of Ten where horrible punishments were meted out to wrong-doers.

In the armoury, amid ranks of fierce weapons, stands a complete suit of armour for a small child, which gives rise to sobering thoughts.

And then, the room of rooms, the **Sala del Maggior Consiglio** (Great Council Chamber). Here, in the early days of genuine democracy, Venice's citizens assembled to elect doges and argue out state policies. Later, only the nobles convened in the vast hall. This was also the scene of a sumptuously appointed banquet for Henry III of France in 1574; 3,000 aristocrats were invited.

Finally, in this room in 1797, the last doge abdicated, and the Venetian republic fell to Napoleon.

Covering the wall behind the doge's throne is the largest oil painting on earth, Tintoretto's *Paradise*. This monumental work, undertaken by the artist at the age of 70, is based on Dante's *Paradiso*.

The portraits of 76 doges, many simply artistic guess-

work, line the cornice beneath the ceiling. The place of Marin Faliero, however, contains a black curtain with the notice that this 14th-century doge was beheaded for treason.

The palace's infamous prisons, which Charles Dickens among others professed to find so dreadful, are disappointing. For the most part, they held only common criminals. Though dark and somewhat evocatively gloomy, the cells are neatly swept out today. Former torture chambers are not on view. Watch your head as you move through the narrow corridors.

The most elaborate prisons **51**

Picturesque Bridge of Sighs once evoked the grimmest forebodings.

sageways, so that prisoners going to the Council of Ten wouldn't meet those who'd already been through the inquisitorial process. From the bridge's grilled windows, prisoners got their only glimpse of the lagoon and *that*, according to a variation on the legend, is why they sighed.

If you visit the palace on your own, you may be able to rent a portable recorder at the entrance. Otherwise, many guided tours are offered, and custodians are pleased to describe the rooms. (See the special section on HOURS on p. 113 for the palace's current schedule.)

San Giorgio Maggiore

A four-minute ride on the *vaporetto* takes you to that inviting little island in the middle of St. Mark's basin, a trip no visitor to Venice should miss. The island and the church are both called San Giorgio Maggiore.

For the very best **view** of Venice proper, go up to the top of the *campanile*. (The 200-year-old tower tilts slightly, but you probably won't even notice.) From here, you can see the canals and, of course, the incomparable Venice sky-

are in another building, connected to the palace by the storied **Ponte dei Sospiri** (Bridge of Sighs). Venetians will tell you that the bridge was unfairly named by anti-Venetian writers who claimed that prisoners sighed as they were led over the enclosed, escape-proof bridge to torture or execution. The Baroque stone bridge, built in the early 17th century, has two parallel pas-

line. There may not be a charge for the lift ride, but most visitors, exhilarated by the view, drop coins in a box for the church's maintenance.

It's certainly worth preserving. Andrea Palladio designed both the church and the adjacent monastery buildings in 1565, creating a masterpiece of proportion and harmonious space. Paintings by Tintoretto, *The Last Supper* and *Gathering of Manna,* grace the high altar.

A small, winding staircase behind the altar leads to a fascinating room. Here, on March 14, 1800, 35 cardinals met in secret conclave to elect Pope Pius VII. Each cardinal's wooden seat is marked—as if they had just left the chamber. The red hat preserved in the display case belonged to the newly elected pope. At the entrance stands the stove where the chamberlain burned the ballot slips.

The monastery, which was an Austrian army barracks during the occupation, now houses the Cini Foundation for study of Venetian civilization. Special permission may be obtained from the foundation to visit the refectory, cloisters and other buildings which are among Palladio's finest achievements.

Many Venice artists spent a lifetime painting only their own city.

The Art of Venice

Accademia
(Academy)

Art lovers spend many days studying this unsurpassed assemblage of Venetian paintings. The average tourist, with time for only one visit, can hardly expect to absorb all the riches displayed in the Accademia. It's certainly better to be selective, rather than trying to see everything and taking in nothing. The following **53**

Mestre

Ponte della Libertà

Canale di Cannaregio

Fondamenta di Cannaregio

Fondamenta Cappuccine

Campo Ghetto Nuovo

Fond.

Tempio Israelitico

GHETTO

R. Terra S. Leonardo

S. Geremia

Pal. Vendramin-Calergi

Scalzi

Canal Grande

Fondaco dei Turchi

Stazione Ferrovia

Ca' Pes

S. Simeone Piccolo

Campo S. Giacomo dell'Orio

Chiara Chiala

S. Fund. S

Scuola S. Giovanni Evangelista

Fond. S. Andrea

Calle della Laca

Campo S. Polo

Piazzale Roma

Can.

San Rocco

S. ta Maria Gloriosa dei Frari

R. di S. Maria Maggiore

R. di S. M. Maggiore

Rio Terra dei Pensieri

Fond. Rio Nuovo

Rio

Canal

Foscari

Campo S. Margherita

Ca' Foscari

Pal. Grassi

C. Carrozze

S. Stefano

Palazzo Rezzonico

Campo Morosin

Scuola dei Carmini

San Nicolò dei Mendicoli

Ponte dell' Accademia

San Sebastiano

Galleria dell' Accademia di Belle Arti

Collezione Guggenheim

Gesuati

Canale della Giudecca

Fondamenta delle Zattere

rundown of the museum's highlights should help.

Any visit to the Accademia must include Veronese's *Feast at the House of Levi*, a compelling canvas which covers an entire wall in Room X. Painted in 1573 as *The Last Supper*, this famous work angered Vatican authorities, who reprimanded Veronese for including "dogs, buffoons, drunken Germans, dwarfs and other such absurdities". Given three months to correct the picture, Veronese simply retitled it. None of the fascinating figures (look for the animals under the table) was removed; the masterpiece remained intact.

In the same room hang Tintoretto's dazzling St. Mark paintings, notably the haunting *Transport of the Body of St. Mark*. Titian's late, dark and sober *Pietà* is also here.

The overpowering Room XI contains Veronese and Tintoretto masterpieces and some memorable Tiepolos—all worth close examination.

Room XX has two of Venice's most famous paintings. Gentile Bellini's *Procession Around the Piazza Bearing the Cross* shows how little San Marco has changed since 1496—except for its mosaics and the addition of the clock tower and Procuratie Nuove to the Piazza. In the second one, Carpaccio's *The Miracle of the Holy Cross at the Rialto Bridge* with its intriguingly familiar gondolas on the Grand Canal, we can see the previous bridge at the Rialto.

Carpaccio's greatly admired *St. Ursula* cycle in Room XXI portrays the King of England and others involved with the tragic young lady.

Presentation by Titian, in Room XXIV, is considered one of the master's finest works.

Far smaller in size but none the less celebrated are the paintings in Rooms IV and V, particularly Mantegna's *St. George*, Giorgone's *Tempest* and Giovanni Bellini's series of the Madonna and Child.

To enjoy these exceptional paintings, of course, means hurrying past dozens of others. Time here is at a premium, however. The Accademia keeps rather restricted hours. Staff shortages and strikes have made it necessary at times to close all or part of the collection a few days each week. The museum's hours (at the time of publication) are given on p. 113, but it is wise to double check at your hotel or the tourist office.

Venetian Artists

Venice's greatest legacy —aside from the city itself—is its painting. JACOPO BELLINI (1400–70) and his sons GIOVANNI (1430–1516) and GENTILE (1429–1507) inaugurated the Serenissima's glorious era of art in the 15th century. The Venetian High Renaissance began with GIORGIONE (1477–1510), and three masters carried it to the supreme heights: TITIAN (1490–1576), JACOPO TINTORETTO (1518–1594) and PAOLO VERONESE (1528–88).

Titian, hailed by many as the greatest painter of his time, is abundantly represented in Venice. Many of his masterworks —brilliantly coloured, dynamic compositions— are at the Frari church (see p. 59). Tintoretto, too, can be seen all over the city but nowhere is his genius more evident than in the glowing series he painted to cover the walls and ceiling of Scuola di San Rocco (see p. 58). Veronese has his own church, San Sebastiano (see p. 63), resplendent with his joyous paintings, and at the Accademia there is his monumental *Feast at the House of Levi*.

The most Venetian of painters, VITTORE CARPACCIO (1445–1526), left us intricately detailed scenes of city life between 1490 and 1526, as well as the narrative series at the Scuola di San Giorgio degli Schiavoni (see p. 58). He influenced ANTONIO CANALETTO (1697–1768), whose views of Venice are reproduced endlessly today throughout the world. Perhaps the finest Venetian decorative painter was GIOVANNI BATTISTA TIEPOLO (1696–1770), on view around Venice but probably most admired for his vast paintings in the Bishop's Residence in Würzburg, Germany, and the royal palace in Madrid.

It's often remarked that only Venetian painters have succeeded in capturing Venice on canvas. Many of Europe's finest artists came and tried, with disappointing results.

Scuola Grande di San Rocco

An absolutely breathtaking collection of Tintoretto's paintings, 56 in all, is displayed here in one of the most opulent interiors imaginable.

Tintoretto covered the gloriously gilded upstairs ceiling with 21 pictures and did 13 more to decorate the walls. What you should do is hire a mirror, by far the *best* way to study the stunning sacred works on the ceiling: *Moses Drawing Water from the Rock*, *The Miracle of Manna* and *Punishments of the Serpents*.

Beneath the murals are some marvellous, if odd, wooden figures by Venice's off-beat 17th-century sculptor, Francesco Pianto. Some impudently mock Tintoretto. The famous spy with a cloak across his face represents Curiosity, should you wonder.

Off the main hall, in the sumptuous Sala dell'Albergo, hangs Tintoretto's monumental *Crucifixion*. He's said to have considered this his greatest painting.

San Rocco, formerly one of the five great Venetian *scuole*, or charitable guilds, charges an admission fee. Though somewhat expensive for a gallery, the masterpieces on view are well worth the price. (Keep your entrance ticket; it must be shown to the custodians at the top of the awesome staircase.)

Scuola di San Giorgio degli Schiavoni

Probably nowhere is so much spectacular painting on view in such a tiny space. This captivating little building was the guildhall of Dalmatian merchants in Venice. At the beginning of the 16th century, these Slavs *(schiavoni)*, prospering from trade with the Levant, commissioned Vittore Carpaccio to decorate their hall. His nine pictures, completed between 1502 and 1508, cover the walls of the ground-floor chapel. Note also the wonderfully ornate wooden ceiling.

Three of Carpaccio's paintings depict St. George (notably killing the dragon), who was *not* English even though he's England's patron saint. He may possibly have been Dalmatian. Also on view here is the famous picture of St. Jerome (unquestionably a Dalmatian and universally revered), sitting in his study with his alert little terrier.

For the hours of San Giorgio, see the special section on p. 113. The friendly custodian is delighted to explain the paintings to visitors who speak Italian.

Santa Maria Gloriosa dei Frari

Known familiarly as I Frari, this is Venice's second church after San Marco (and more or less a sister of San Zanipolo, another Gothic giant across the city). Here you will find two of Titian's most famous paintings—the stunning *Assumption* (1518) above the Frari's high altar and the *Madonna of Ca' Pesaro* (1526), which graces an altar on the left, evidently representing the artist's own wife. A third masterpiece on view here is Giovanni Bellini's 1488 triptych of the *Madonna and Saints* at the sacristy altar.

Donatello's much-loved wooden statue of *St. John the Baptist,* its colours brilliantly restored during the 19th century, dominates the chapel to the right of the main altar. A "must" for photographers.

On opposite sides of the Frari's great nave you will find the huge tombs of Titian and sculptor Antonio Canova. Titian's was erected by the Emperor of Austria, 300 years after the artist's death.

This immense, lofty church was built between 1340 and

Glowing interior of I Frari, the church where Titian is buried.

1469 for the Franciscan friars; its seven chapels are crammed with art and tombs. A token entrance fee is charged, except during mass.

Collezione Guggenheim

American expatriate Peggy Guggenheim, who died in 1979, left behind one of the

*Taking time out for a break—
a favourite Venetian pastime.*

best comprehensive collections of modern art in Europe. It remains in her 18th-century home on the Grand Canal, Palazzo Venier dei Leoni—a rare opportunity for tourists to get inside one of those Venetian palaces.

The collection is now administered by New York's Solomon Guggenheim Foundation, which has refurbished the house and turned it into an official museum. Among the outstanding offerings: a 1910 cubist painting by Picasso, *The Poet*, and Constantine Brancusi's often-imitated bronze sculpture, *Bird in Flight*. The

curator calls Marino Marini's bold bronze horse and rider, which stares through the gate at the Grand Canal, "our pride and joy".

Other artists represented include Marcel Duchamp, Max Ernst, Miró, Mondrian and Jackson Pollock (a whole roomful).

The Palazzo Venier is open to the public from April to October.

Madonna dell'Orto
(of the garden)

Often referred to as the city's "English church", since money for the restoration of its outstanding art works came from the English people, more properly, it belongs to Tintoretto. It was the great Renaissance artist's parish church, and he is buried with his family near the high altar. It also contains two of his finest paintings. Soaring 50 feet up each side of the high altar are Tintoretto's *Last Judgment* and *The Worship of the Golden Calf*, which have dazzled onlookers for four centuries. His dramatic *Presentation of the Virgin* over the sacristy door is also greatly admired.

Look also for Cima da Conegliano's remarkable painting of *St. John the Baptist* to the right of the entrance.

This church, with its striking Gothic façade and delightful cloister, was erected in the 15th century in the quiet northern quarter of Cannaregio to house another miraculous statue of the Virgin and Child, found in a nearby garden *(orto)*. Strategically located across the canal in front of the church is a leading Venetian undertaker; frequently one or two black funeral boats trimmed with gold lions are moored outside.

and covering its arched ceiling with portraits of holy men. The Miracoli was built for and named after the picture of the Virgin Mary at the towering altar, one of a number of medieval religious portraits in Venice credited with miraculous healing.

The afternoon, when sunshine streaming through the

The exquisite Miracoli, cherished by generations of Venice visitors.

More Memorable Churches

🚶 Santa Maria dei Miracoli

Venetians call this their "golden jewel box" *(scrigno d'oro)*, and like to get married here. Some enthusiasts call it the most beautiful church in the world.

Though difficult to find in the warren of canals and narrow walkways behind the Rialto Bridge, Santa Maria dei Miracoli enchants even the most indifferent church visitor. Those pioneers of early-Renaissance architecture, the Lombardo family, built this surprisingly small church between 1481 and 1489, marbling the inner and outer walls

windows glints off the gilt ceiling, is the best time to see the Miracoli. The custodian will turn on the lights for close inspection of the remarkable carved figures decorating the choir stalls and the entire chancel. You may not visit the church during religious services.

Washday in Venice: a reminder that the city is not just a museum.

Though not on the main tourist itinerary, this is one of the true treasures of Venice; to sit quietly in a pew when the Miracoli is uncrowded is an unforgettable experience.

The church dominates its immediate neighbourhood: one photo shop proudly displays pictures of the latest crop of beaming brides and nervous-looking grooms, blissfully ignoring the Renaissance splendour of the Miracoli.

San Sebastiano

Purportedly the best-restored church in Venice, San Sebastiano is a glittering tribute to that much-loved painter Veronese, who is buried here among many of his works. It was built in 1548 to commemorate the end of a plague.

Veronese painted most of the colourful, sensuous works decorating the walls, altar and fantastic ceiling. For a small sum "to cover our electricity bill", the custodian will be glad to turn on the lights which, with the handy viewing mirror, is the only way to really see one of Venice's most beautiful churches.

San Nicolò dei Mendicoli

Often overlooked way down behind the docks, this humble parish church, erected in the 7th century, is one of Venice's gems. The campanile of San Nicolò has stood for 800 years; noisy children are admonished to be quiet or it will fall down.

The candle-lit interior conveys an entrancingly ancient

atmosphere. Its beautiful madonnas and gilt arches have been carefully restored by the British Venice in Peril Fund.

SS. Giovanni e Paolo*

Almost 200 years passed between the time work started on this huge brick church and its consecration in 1430. Ever since, it has had a very special

---

* Although formally named Santi Giovanni e Paolo, many Venetians will not understand unless you ask for San Zanipolo—another curious local convention.

Bartolomeo Colleoni paid in advance for his own fine statue.

place in Venetian hearts. One of the city's two great Gothic churches (with the Frari), it is commonly known as the Pantheon of Venice because so many doges and lesser republican dignitaries are buried here.

Art experts argue about the comparative merits of Giovanni Bellini's very early polyptych (right-hand nave) and Lorenzo Lotto's mellow-toned *St. Anthony*. But it's the tombs, some with graphically morbid sculptures, that dominate the church, often arousing strong emotions.

In the *campo* (small square) outside proudly stands the

15th-century masterpiece by Andrea Verrocchio and Alessandro Leopardi, probably the world's most famous **equestrian statue.** The rider, assertive in glimmering green,

A familiar landmark on the Grand Canal, Santa Maria della Salute.

was Bartolomeo Colleoni, a mercenary captain who left money for a statue of himself, stipulating that it should be erected in the Piazza San Marco. The republic did not ordinarily erect monuments to contemporary figures, but hated to waste the money; it shrewdly decided to put Colleoni's statue outside the Scuola di San Marco instead (now Venice's municipal hospital), next to San Zanipolo.

Santa Maria della Salute

For 300 years, this magnificent Venetian Baroque church has guarded the entrance to the Grand Canal, its huge dome radiating proud splendour. Baldassare Longhena, the architect, erected the massive octagonal structure on more than one million sunken oak pilings, each 12 feet long.

The Salute was built to thank the Virgin Mary for the end of a catastrophic plague in 1630 (see p. 19). Since 1670, Venice has been celebrating the Festa della Salute on November 21; engineers build a bridge of boats over the Grand Canal, and most of the city walks across and up into the church. Its main doors open only on this holiday.

Inside, in the sacristy to the left of the high altar, hangs **65**

Venetian fishermen still bring in fresh fish daily for your table.

Tintoretto's great *Marriage at Cana.* A number of Titians, including *The Sacrifice of Abraham, Cain and Abel* and *David and Goliath* are to be found there as well.

Earlier this century, the Salute had a notice warning "angels falling". But the masonry has since been repaired and the art work beautifully restored by the French, who have taken a special interest in this beloved Venetian landmark.

Venice Past and Present

Museo Correr

To gain an overall impression of Venice past and present, there's no easier or more interesting way than to spend a few hours in this remarkable museum. Commencing dramatically at the top of imperial stairs in the Napoleonic wing, the Correr runs along two sides of the Piazza. It offers a fascinating assortment of Veniciana—crimson doges' robes, priceless old maps of the city (look for Jacopo de Barbari's captivating wood engraving of Venice in 1500 near the entrance), election documents and vivid portraits of many doges, coins minted over the centuries, a memorably musty library, spears and armour, naval cannon and models of galleys. On the upper level, an art gallery contains delightful Carpaccios, Bellinis and Lorenzo Lottos. The adjacent small museum of the Risorgimento illustrates Venice's history since the fall of the republic.

The Correr has added recently an extremely useful section for visitors: magnified colour photographs of the city's major attractions are displayed side by side with paintings by the masters depicting the same scenes in past centuries. It's astonishing how little Venice has changed.

The collection was left to the city in 1830 by Teodoro Correr, a member of one of Venice's oldest noble families.

Ghetto

For almost 300 years, until Napoleon ended the practice in 1797, the Jews of Venice were forced to live in this canal-surrounded section of Cannaregio which gives its name to Jewish quarters all over the world. Most experts believe *ghetto* comes from the verb *gettare,* to cast in metal, because of the district's foundries. Other possible origins are the old rabbinical word *ghet* (separation) and a Syrian word *nghetto* (congregation).

From the 12th century, Jews inhabited—and presumably gave their name to—the island of Giudecca, the nearby mainland and later all of Venice. But, in 1516, the senate restricted them to Cannaregio.

Jewish refugees from Spain and central Europe poured into the Venice ghetto where the limited space produced tenements six storeys high, still among the city's tallest

buildings. Though severely taxed, forced to wear distinctive yellow clothing and denied the right to practise many professions, the Jews of Venice generally suffered no physical harassment. For a time, many of the republic's financial activities were even concentrated in the Ghetto, bringing an unusual spell of prosperity.

Today the Ghetto is one of the poorest districts in Venice—a far cry from the image presented by Shakespeare in *The Merchant of Venice*.

Ca' (or) Palazzo Rezzonico

Call it a house or a palace (Venetians do both), the Rezzonico is one of the most magnificent residences imaginable. To wander through it is not so much to tour a museum as to be transported back to a grand home of the 18th century. A plaque on one corner notes that Robert Browning died here on December 12, 1889; he who wrote:

Open my heart and you will see

Graved inside of it, Italy.

Restored by American gifts, the Rezzonico fascinates every visitor.

Browning's son Pen bought the palace last century, long after the Rezzonico family had it so magnificently decorated. For the past 40 years, it's been a municipal museum of 18th-century Veniciana.

The startling ballroom at the top of the vast entrance staircase features two immense chandeliers and wildly colourful ceiling and walls. In the small rooms adjacent to the ballroom, look for the intricate carvings of Negro figures.

On the second floor, there are some splendid paintings of 18th-century Venice. The top floor, not always open, contains some delightful puppets. Many visitors linger at the windows for one of the best views along the Grand Canal.

See the special section on HOURS on p. 113 of this book.

Quayside artists specialize in local scenes and instant portraits.

Riva degli Schiavoni
(Quay of the Slavs)

Before, in-between or after more formal sightseeing, don't miss a stroll along the magnificent *riva* which curves gently away from San Marco. The world has few more famous or stately waterfronts.

Starting at the Doges' Palace, the Riva degli Schiavoni is named after those industrious Dalmatian (Slav) merchants whose boats used to tie up here laden with Eastern wares. The Riva changes its name several times as it sweeps around St. Mark's basin to the public gardens installed by Napoleon. From there, you can enjoy a glorious panoramic view of the whole of Venice.

The pleasant church of Santa Maria della Pietà had Antonio Vivaldi, Venice's musical giant, as its concert master from 1705 to 1740. Henry James took a room on the Riva and did some writing. Charles Dickens stayed at the **69**

Take a stroll along the banks of the Grand Canal or just take a seat and watch the world pass by.

famous Hotel Danieli near the Doges' Palace, and many celebrities since have followed his example.

You'll invariably find much to look at on the busy Riva: sea-going tugs and scores of gondolas, cruise ships and weather-beaten fishing boats, landscape painters and quick-sketch artists setting up easels around King Victor Emmanuel II's statue, hawkers selling *frittelle* (Venetian doughnuts).

Marco Polo

Venice's most famous citizen opened the eyes of 13th-century Europe to the irresistibly exotic mysteries of the Orient. For some 20 years, Marco Polo served the Mongol Emperor Kublai Khan. He was the first Westerner permitted to travel about freely in China.

Maps in the Doges' Palace trace Polo's voyages which opened up new routes for the spice trade. When he came back from China, legend has it that no one recognized him or believed his tales—that is, until the returning hero slit the seams of his clothing and precious jewels fell out.

For many centuries, schoolchildren learned of the East from Marco Polo's book of travels *(Il Milione)*. You may be told (and it may be true) that he brought the recipe for pasta back to Venice from China. Others suggest it was Marco Polo who introduced pasta to Peking.

And Venetian blinds? Some believe Marco brought the idea from the East, where the thin wooden slats had been in use for many centuries. Or, again, perhaps he took "Venetian blinds" to the East with him. Nobody's really sure: in Italian, Venetian blinds are called *persiane alla veneziana,* or simply *persiane* (shutters).

Arsenale

This was the greatest shipyard in the world. For 700 years before Napoleon, the republic's galleys and galleons were built here. Dante visited it and thought the place was like the Inferno. But the Arsenal's 16,000 masters and builders were highly respected citizens, even if they had to toil amid vapours of boiling pitch.

Arsenale, meaning house of industry, is another of those Venetian words that have passed into many other languages. The yard also passed along the idea of a conveyor-belt system: newly built galleys were fitted out by being towed simultaneously past supply storehouses. It was incredibly fast and efficient.

One of Venice's proudest tales concerns the shipyard. When Henry III of France was **71** visiting in the 16th century, a state banquet was arranged in his honour. To impress him, the Arsenal turned out one completely equipped galley while the king was eating his dinner.

Today the Arsenal is a rather sleepy Italian naval yard. Visitors *on foot* get no further than the beautifully restored triumphal arch at the entrance, the finest example of early-Renaissance architecture in Venice. But if you take the No. 5 *vaporetto,* you sail right through.

Museo Storico Navale
(Naval History Museum)

A "must" for sea lovers, maritime-history buffs and children of all ages, this three-storey nautical collection provides a nice change from the standard Venetian fare of churches and art galleries. Among the more unexpected attractions is a roomful of marvellous models of Chinese junks, donated in 1964 by a French admirer of Marco Polo. See p. 113 for the museum's hours.

Lido

Celebrated and imitated the world over, the Lido is in fact much more important as a barrier island protecting Venice than as a beach resort of long-faded glamour. The word itself simply means beach or shore, and in Venice, the *lidi* are the sand bars or reefs separating the lagoon from the Adriatic.

With swimming in that murky sea still officially permitted, much of the Lido's

seven-mile-long beach strip is umbrellaed and parcelled off by the busy hotels and municipal establishments, leaving little beach space for those who venture over from Venice proper.

It's all a far cry from the days of the doges, when nobles hunted in the Lido's woods and grassy wastes or rode horses along its deserted shore. Lord Byron loved to walk on the Lido. It was from the San Nicolò end that he began his celebrated swimming race, which ended without his two competitors at the far end of the Grand Canal.

Admirers of Thomas Mann seeking that *Death in Venice* atmosphere will be disappointed during the summer and early autumn. In season, the strip is boisterously alive with tourists, film-festival fans, earnest golfers and speed-boat enthusiasts. After October, though, when the crowds have disappeared and the first mists and fog banks seep in from the sea, the Lido does take on a rather funereal air.

Express and ordinary *vaporetti* run back and forth between Venice and the Lido, gondolas can be hired, and there are several car ferries to the island, where driving is permitted.

For those full of Venice's romance with the sea, it's worth a bus trip and walk to the northern end of the island to see the Porto di Lido, the lagoon's main passageway to the Adriatic. Here doges "wed" the sea yearly in that most spectacular of Serenissima ceremonies (see p. 8). And through this gateway passed all the republic's battle and trade fleets before striking out on the open sea.

Excursions

A highlight of any visit to Venice is, of course, venturing out onto that inviting lagoon. You can see the three most popular islands in a leisurely one-day outing or can make half-day trips to one or more of them.

Venetians go to the islands by *vaporetto*. The Nos. 5 or 12 will take you out to Murano in about 15 minutes. After some sightseeing, you can continue on to Burano and Torcello by public transport. Guided tours by steamer or motorboat—and privately hired gondolas—are, of course, more expensive.

73

Artisans create fanciful animals of glass before your very eyes.

Anyone spending more than a few days in Venice should try to make a tour of its mainland **villas.** It was fashionable, in the 15th and 16th centuries for aristocrats to have country houses. Many are architectural gems, particularly those by Andrea Palladio. If you take the nostalgic boat trip to **Padua** (on a modern version of the historic *burchiello*, or barge, which operates from May to September), you'll see more villas, as well as a famous set of Giotto frescoes and the superb equestrian statue by Donatello. And Palladio's home town of **Vicenza** is filled with fine examples of the master's work.

Murano

This sprawling island, less than a mile north of Venice, is actually a cluster of five islets. Its name is synonymous the world over with Venetian glassware—unfortunately, not what it used to be.

Glass was manufactured in Venice as far back as the 10th century, but the open furnaces presented such a fire hazard that, in 1292, the doge ordered the glass factories transferred out to Murano. Grouped together here, the glass blowers kept their secrets for centuries. Making mirrors, for instance, was long a Venetian exclusivity. The Muranese probably invented eye glasses, and they made the largest and clearest window panes in Europe. The island prospered: its population reached 30,000, its crystal ware decorated royal palaces abroad and its villas housed the leading nobles and diplomats of Venice.

As other countries eventually learned and applied Murano's secrets, the island's importance declined. But last century the glass trade was revived and continues today, although not up to its old standards. Murano's glass museum *(Museo Vetrario),* recently restored, contains

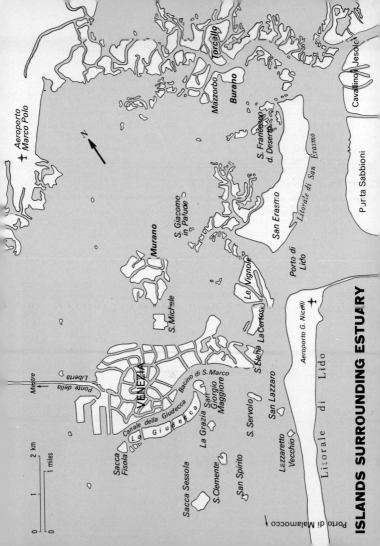

ISLANDS SURROUNDING ESTUARY

Aeroporto Marco Polo

Mestre

Ponte della Libertà

N

Sacca Fisola

Sacca Sessola

S. Clemente

San Spirito

La Giudecca

Canale della Giudecca

VENEZIA

San Giorgio Maggiore

La Grazia

S. Servolo

S. Clemente

San Lazzaro

Lazzaretto Vecchio

S. Michele

Murano

S. Giacomo in Paluce

Le Vignole

S. Elena

La Certosa

Aeroporto G. Nicelli

Bacino di S. Marco

Litorale di Lido

Porto di Malamocco

Mazzorbo

Torcello

Burano

S. Francesco d. Deserto

San Erasmo

Litorale di San Erasmo

Porto di Lido

P.unta Sabbioni

Cavallino Jesolo

0   1   2 km
0   1 miles

many examples of local craftsmanship, some 500 years old.

Hawkers wave people into the factories for a free look at the glass-blowing. A few interesting moments then often turn into high-pressure sales tactics.

Actually, the island's most celebrated attraction is a church, some say the oldest church in Venice. The foundations of Santi Maria e Donato, commonly known as **San Donato,** may go back to the 7th century, predating San Marco. The present building and its commanding bell tower date from the 12th century. San Donato's magnificent mosaic floor and a golden mosaic of the Madonna over the high altar have recently been restored.

🏃 Burano

This absolutely delightful little island is the pearl of the Venetian lagoon, one of the few spots in Europe that haven't changed for the worse over the centuries. From a distance, Burano stands out because of its dramatically tilted bell tower. Closer in, you see a marvellous array of colours: Burano's trim little houses are painted blue, red, green, russet with no rhyme or reason. The

effect is part of the island's charm. Nicknamed the "Montparnasse of Venice", it attracts droves of painters.

Burano once produced the world's finest lace, its famous *punto in aria* pattern was the most sought after in Europe. Today Buranese women still sit outdoors working on the delicate pillow lace, and a small school teaches techniques dating back at least 400 years. Though a few tables near the boat station may sell lace items, this sleepy island has none of Murano's hard-sell commercialism.

Burano's only "sight" is *Calvary* by Giambattista Tie-

polo, in the parish church of San Martino. Its leaning *campanile*, Buranese will assure you, will stand for centuries.

It takes no more than an hour to wander all round the island. But loiter a bit. You may want to watch the fishermen, who sail right up the little canals and park by their front doors, mending their nets or scraping their boats. Burano has several restaurants specializing in seafood, and a few pleasant outdoor cafés.

Away from the hustle and bustle, Burano's simplicity is welcome.

For a negotiable fee, a boatman will take you over to the island of **San Francesco del Deserto,** with its monastery garden tended by Franciscan friars; legend says St. Francis went aground there once. This side trip takes perhaps an hour and a half and should get you back to Burano after most of the visitors have gone—the best time to savour its tranquillity.

Torcello

There's scarcely a trace of it today, but for ten centuries this overgrown and almost uninhabited island was a thriving

Exquisite Virgin and Child *mosaic glows in the cathedral of Torcello.*

clogged with silt from mainland rivers, and the population was nearly wiped out by malaria and other epidemics. In time, Torcello was abandoned, looted and almost forgotten. The cathedral, the small Santa Fosca church and a few nearby buildings are all the civilization that remains on this island Ruskin called the "mother of Venice".

A short, pleasant walk from the boat landing brings you to "downtown Torcello", population perhaps three dozen. When you enter the **cathedral,** you may catch your breath at the burst of beauty, so unexpected out on this remote island. Most impressive are the blue and gold mosaics of a tearful *Virgin and Child* and the *Apostles* in the apse, Byzantine masterpieces executed some 900 years ago. Experts say that in Italy only Ravenna possesses finer mosaics.

Almost as old, though heavily restored, is the huge mosaic of the *Last Judgment* covering an entire wall of the church. The altar and some of the mosaics date back to the 7th century, the marble floor to the 11th. The 18 columns of veined marble are of Greek origin, the chipped holy-water basin and carved sarcophagus are Roman.

community with as many as 20,000 residents. Long before they settled Venice, mainlanders fleeing barbarians took refuge on Torcello. In 639, a refugee bishop erected the Cathedral of Santa Maria Assunta to house his relics.

For many centuries an independent trading and shipbuilding power, with many splendid homes and churches, Torcello declined as Venice **78** grew. Its canals became

Shopping

Venice offers a dazzling concentration of shops with enticing window displays. A highly style-conscious city, Venice's quality items rival those of Florence or Paris. However, there inevitably is a great amount of junk, glass bric-à-brac and cheap souvenirs.

As a rule, the finest, most expensive shops are around the Piazza. Along Venice's main shopping street, the Merceria, which runs from the clock tower towards the Rialto, you'll find excellent shops with more competitive prices. For more economical if slightly less elegant clothes, most Venetians shop around the Rialto and along the Strada Nuova which leads to the railway station.

While Florence is somewhat better for *major* leather purchases, and Rome's prices for leather and silk goods may be fractionally lower, you won't go far wrong buying either of these Italian standbys in Venice.

Costume jewellery abounds in Venice at reasonable prices; elaborate gold and silver pieces, including some marvellous filigree, may be somewhat more expensive than in northern Europe but show the stamp of Venetian craftsmanship.

Just off San Marco (Calle Larga), it's worth stopping by Venezia Artigiana, an exhibition of ceramics, glass mosaics and jewellery by the city's leading craftsmen. The works are on sale.

What's your fancy—kid gloves, golden chains or a crystal goblet?

Though many shops say they'll ship your packages anywhere abroad, bear in mind the uncertainties of Italy's postal system!

Worth Buying

Leather: Gloves, bags, belts, jackets, coats, book bindings, desk sets and shoes (Italian shoes, normally wider to fit the native foot, have no A, B or C gradings).

Silk: Scarves, shawls, dresses, blouses, shirts, suits, ties.

Masks: A few traditional artisans around town still make those wonderful 17th- or 18th-century theatrical and carnival masks of papier-mâché *(cartapesta).* These are fine souvenirs and certain conversation stoppers.

Old prints, reproductions, maps: You can find many wonderful scenes of the city from its republican era to the present at art or picture-framing shops. Prints or maps of old Venice are astonishingly cheap and easily rolled up in cardboard cylinders for mailing or carrying.

Gondolier's slippers: Normally made of velvet, with rope soles, this must be the ultimate (if a bit hard to find) Venetian gift—unless you can afford a gondola.

Art: Venice, perhaps more than any other city, seems to be by, of, and for artists. Rarely will you see so much painting, drawing, sculpture, pottery and handicrafts for sale in one place. There are galleries here which buy from and sell to millionaires, others which deal in inexpensive pop posters. Street (that is, quay- or canal-side) artists sell their pictures day and night. Portraitists do instant charcoal drawings while you pose in the Piazza or on the Molo, charging what they think you can afford.

Pipes: It's worth asking your hotel porter where you might find clay fishermen's pipes, a charming and off-beat item typical of the Venice lagoon. The original Chioggia type is the most admired.

Hats: An inexpensive, authentic and colourful souvenir is a gondolier's straw hat. Be sure that it has a coloured band.

Approach with Caution

Glass: The Murano glassware (see p. 74) that you see today—and see it you will, all over Venice—is not up to the old standards. But with patience, the discerning buyer may find a nice piece—perhaps a lovely crystal or

You'll be a hit at your next fancydress ball with a Venetian mask.

smoked glass decanter and some stunning drinking glasses. Not surprisingly, these are very expensive, and there's always the risk of their being broken on the way home.

Italianate antiques: Tourists who aren't specialists should beware of locally produced "Victorian" pieces or 1980 copies of 18th-century items. Hawkers of "original" religious relics should also be sternly avoided.

Bargaining

Though a popular pastime in much of Italy, bargaining here will probably be fruitless. The Venetians have been perfect- **81** ing the art of taking other people's money for centuries, and even while smiling broadly, they stick doggedly to their prices—which you *think* are too high, which they *know* are too high, but which are almost never going to come down.

However, out of season you may be able to negotiate a lower price with artists and craftsmen or even in some smaller shops.

Discounts as sales gimmicks are a rarity in Venice. But if you're making a major purchase, try suggesting that the final price be "rounded off". It might work, even in the fanciest shops. Discount is *sconto*.

Even if bargaining is second nature to you, plan to finish last here.

Wining and Dining

Venetians, like other Italians, tend to make an enthusiastic production of any restaurant meal. That means taking at least an hour to eat, probably closer to two, and consuming three or more courses. For much of the year, you can dine outdoors, enjoying both the food and the passing parade.

Though not one of Italy's gastronomic capitals, Venice does have a selection of popular national dishes as well as its own distinctive, often delicious recipes. Best of all is the fact that excellent seafood is available everywhere in Venice.*

Proceeding through the meal Italian style: Venetian restaurants offer a great variety of first courses, such as antipasto of mixed seafood (*misto* or *frutti di mare*) or shrimp (*gamberetti*); crabs (*granzeole*) in the shell; marinated sardines with onions (*sarde in saor*); fish, bean or tripe soup (*zuppa* or *minestra di pesce, fagioli, trippa*); ham (*prosciutto*) with melon or figs (*melone* or *fichi*); or various sausages (*salsicce*).

---

* For a comprehensive glossary of Italian wining and dining, ask your bookshop for the Berlitz EUROPEAN MENU READER.

Summer dining in Venice is often out of doors and quite casual.

Many diners skip this course, commencing in the Italian manner with a rice dish *(risotto)* or pasta. Venice is noted for its *risotto*, which may be made with minced fresh vegetables *(primavera)*, with cuttlefish and its ink *(nero di seppie)*, or with shrimp, chicken livers *(fegatini di pollo)*, spinach *(spinaci)*, asparagus *(asparagi)* or that famous local speciality, rice with peas *(risi e bisi)*.

Spaghetti and many of the other types of Italian pasta are, of course, served in Venice, but generally without much enthusiasm and with far fewer sauces than in Rome or Bologna. But you can enjoy that old north Italian speciality *pasta e fagioli* (pasta and white bean soup) enlivened with garlic. Otherwise, pasta hasn't taken firm root in Venetian kitchens: this is really rice country.

In the game season, you may be urged to try a special dish from the Treviso area called *sopa coada;* this is a thick, savoury mixture of pigeon and bread baked slowly and served as a first course.

The variety of wonderfully edible creatures from the Adriatic seems infinite here. Perhaps the local favourite is eel *(anguilla)*, often served *alla veneziana*—cooked in a lemon, oil and tunny-fish 83 sauce. Almost every restaurant offers fillets of John Dory (*San Piero* or *Sampiero*), a tasty white fish prepared however you prefer, and a delicious if strangely named fish *coda di rospo,* literally, toad's tail, its lobster-like texture best grilled so that it has a slightly burned taste. You'll also find dried salt cod *(baccalà)* usually creamed, gilthead bream *(orata),* Adriatic sole *(sfogio* or *sogliola)* which may be served in a sweet-and-sour sauce *(in saor),* sea bass *(spigola* or *branzino)* and prawns *(scampi).*

Many restaurants offer their own *gran fritto misto,* a deep-fried selection that may include sole, scampi, eel and squid. Garnished with lemon slices and accompanied by a mixed salad—perhaps with fennel *(finocchio),* a popular ingredient locally—this is a summer lunch hard to beat.

Meat is much less to be recommended in Venice, although calves' liver and onions *(fegato alla veneziana)* is done with great finesse. Veal *(vitello),* the Italian national meat, comes in its usual varieties. An ordinary beefsteak *(filetto di bue)* is likely to be just that—ordinary; Florentine T-bone steak *(bistecca alla fiorentina),* is Italy's best beef, if you can find it. Pork *(maiale),* often seen on menus, can be delicious. Lamb *(agnello),* not too common in Venice, is always a good bet.

Polenta, the omnipresent side dish, is a firm, yellow maize purée, rather bland to non-Venetian palates, but absolutely essential from the local point of view. Though not always mentioned on the menu, it often appears on your plate.

From the foothills around Bassano come wonderful white asparagus to enliven the tables of Venice, and from the Veneto's mountain area come mushrooms *(funghi)* of all shapes and sizes. Grilled giant boletus mushrooms (*porcini* or *brise)* are relished as a main course. Artichokes *(carciofi),* justifiably popular in season, are best Roman style *(alla Romana)*—cooked through so every bit may be eaten.

Most of the well-known Italian cheeses are available at better restaurants, including the blue *gorgonzola,* the bland *bel paese* and the piquant *parmigiano,* the last eaten not only grated for soups and pastas but in chunks after a meal. Among the Veneto province delicacies is a tangy goat's milk cheese named after the mountain town Asiago.

As elsewhere in Italy, an inviting selection of fruit is offered to round off your meal. Watch for blood oranges from Sicily.

For those still able to summon an appetite for dessert, restaurants always have several flavours of that unrivalled Italian ice-cream and a choice of tarts or cakes *della casa* (of the house). The famous *zuppa inglese,* a sort of creamy trifle of custard and liquored sponge cake, is Italian, not English, and has nothing remotely to do with soup.

Mineral water *(acqua minerale),* carbonated *(gasata)* or still *(naturale),* is an article of faith with Italians who insist it not only aids digestion but has a host of other more meaningful medical properties as well. Though Venice's tap water is perfectly drinkable, it's a good idea to have a bottle of *minerale* with a meal—not only to humour the natives, but because it honestly does help ease all that food down.

And, of course, you'll find a second glass (the smaller one) in front of you for wine. Venetian area whites and reds are perfectly acceptable but not outstanding, regardless of price, so you might just as well order a carafe of open wine and save money. A good, all-purpose rosé is Pinot Grigio from the nearby Treviso area—a brand name better known as a white wine.

The best Veneto reds, usually only by the bottle, include Valpolicella, Bardolino and Cabernet, while Merlot from nearby Friuli-Venezia Giulia is also respected. Good whites available in Venice include Soave from Verona, Gambellara, Prosecco and the well-known Tocai, again from the neighbouring province.

Among the finer Italian red wines you may find Chianti from Tuscany, Barolo and Gattinara from the Piedmont area and Sangiovese from Emilia-Romagna. The best whites include Vermentino from Sardinia (rare, but worth looking for) and some of the Riesling-type wines of the Trentino-Alto Adige mountain country.

Before dinner, you can enjoy one of the noted Italian *aperitivi*—Campari, Punt e Mes, Cinzano or another red or white vermouth. Any of these will be dramatically cheaper than foreign cocktails.

Among the most favoured Italian after-dinner drinks are the sweet yellowish Strega, the powerful green Cent'erbe, the mildly bitter Amaro or

Amaretto, the syrupy, anise-flavoured Sambuca (served by superstition only with an odd number of coffee beans) and a variety of passable brandies. At the end of your meal, you may well be offered one of these *digestivi* without charge by the restaurant owner, an appealing custom still practised in Italy.

From Tavola Calda to Ristorante

You'll find everything in Venice from stand-up snack bars *(tavola calda)* to deluxe restaurants—almost all rather expensive by Italian standards. There are, of course, *pizzerie* for a sit-down pizza or, if you're in a hurry, places selling pizza by the slice. Bars and cafés almost always have a selection of sandwiches *(tramezzini),* inexpensive if you eat at the counter. For those with an international student identity card, two restaurants in Campo Santa Margherita serve inexpensive meals.

The *tavola calda,* an omnipresent Italian institution, serves up from a counter and steam-table more substantial "snacks" such as a plate of pasta, stuffed marrow *(zucchini ripieni),* hamburgers, roast veal, perhaps deep-fried fish.

There may be some tables and chairs, but no waiter service; normally you must eat standing up, jostled at peak hours by dozens of Venetians doing the same thing. The food should be acceptable, the price vastly lower than in proper restaurants. In the same vein, Venice has a few self-service restaurants.

A small, probably family-run restaurant is often called a *trattoria* or, in Venice, also a *locanda.* The city has 225 such places. Here you'll find a rather basic menu—perhaps half a dozen rice, pasta or soup starters, the same number of fish and meat dishes, salad, cheese, fruit and ice-cream. Outstanding cuisine in such places is a great rarity in Venice, but one normally eats decently if unimaginatively.

Venice's 46 regular *ristorante,* which may also be nicknamed *trattorie* or *locande,* feature elaborate menus, elaborate table settings and elaborate prices.

Most restaurants offer a *menù turistico,* a fixed-price three- or four-course meal with limited choice.

All restaurants, no matter how modest, must now issue a formal receipt indicating the tax (I.V.A.). A customer may actually be stopped outside the premises and fined if he is unable to produce a receipt. The bill usually includes cover *(coperto)* and service *(servizio)* charges, but it's customary to leave an additional 500 lire or so per person. Never tip the restaurant owner, even if he has showered you with attention.

Whether your whim is fish or fowl, Venetian cuisine can fill the bill.

To Help You Order...

Good evening. I'd like a table for three. **Buona sera. Vorrei un tavolo per tre persone.**

Could we have a table outside? **Potremmo avere un tavolo all'esterno?**

Do you have a set menu? **Avete un menù a prezzo fisso?**

I'd like a/an/some... **Vorrei...**

ashtray	**un portacenere**	mineral water	**dell'acqua minerale**
beer	**una birra**		
bread	**del pane**	napkin	**un tovagliolo**
butter	**del burro**	olive oil	**dell'olio d'oliva**
chair	**una sedia**	pepper	**del pepe**
coffee	**un caffè**	potatoes	**delle patate**
condiments	**del condimento**	salad	**dell'insalata**
cream	**della panna**	salt	**del sale**
cutlery	**delle posate**	sandwich	**un sandwich**
dessert	**un dessert**	serviette	**un tovagliolo**
fish	**del pesce**	soup	**una minestra**
fork	**una forchetta**	spoon	**un cucchiaio**
fruit	**della frutta**	sugar	**dello zucchero**
glass	**un bicchiere**	tea	**un tè**
ice-cream	**un gelato**	toothpick	**uno stuzzica-denti**
knife	**un coltello**		
meat	**della carne**	(iced) water	**dell'acqua (fredda)**
menu	**un menù**		
milk	**del latte**	wine	**del vino**

...and Read the Menu

aglio	garlic	**antipasto**	hors d'œuvre
albicocche	apricots	**arancia**	orange
anguilla	eel	**arrosto**	roast
anguria	watermelon	**baccalà**	dried cod
anitra	duck	**bigoli***	fat noodle

88

bisato*	eel	**melanzana**	aubergine (egg-plant)
braciola	chop		
branzino	sea bass	**merluzzo**	cod
brodetto	fish soup	**minestra**	soup
calamari	squid	**peperoni**	peppers, pimentos
carciofi	artichokes		
cervello fritto	deep-fried brains	**pesca**	peach
		pesce	fish
cicoria	endive (Am. chicory)	**pesce spada**	swordfish
		pesse*	fish
cipolle	onions	**polenta**	purée of maize (cornmeal)
coniglio	rabbit		
cozze	mussels	**pollo**	chicken
crostacei	shellfish	**prosciutto**	ham
dentice	dentex (a white fish)	**(e melone o fichi)**	(with melon or figs)
fagiano	pheasant	**quaglia**	quail
fagioli	beans	**risi e bisi**	rice and peas
faraona	guinea fowl	**risotto**	rice dish
fasoi*	beans	**rognoni**	kidneys
fegato alla veneziana	liver and onions	**salsa**	sauce
		saor*	vinegar sauce
fichi	figs	**seppia**	cuttlefish
formaggio	cheese	**sfogio***	sole
fragole	strawberries	**sogliola**	sole
fritto	fried	**sopa***	soup
frutti di mare	seafood	**spigola**	sea bass
		spinaci	spinach
funghi	mushrooms	**stufato**	stew
gamberi	scampi, prawns	**triglia**	red mullet
		trippe	tripe
gnocchi	dumplings	**uova**	eggs
granceole*	shellfish	**vitello**	veal
insalata	salad	**vitello tonnato**	veal (cold) braised in a sauce of tuna, mayonnaise, capers
lamponi	raspberries		
lombata di maiale	pork tender-loin		
luganega	pork sausage	**vongole**	clams
mela	apple	**zuppa**	soup

* Venetian dialect

Relaxing in Venice

To beat the heat or ease sore feet, there's nothing like a leisurely drink or an ice-cream at an outdoor café. Practically every *campo,* or square, in Venice has one, and in Italian fashion, you won't be hurried if you spend hours sitting there without ordering anything beyond that first coffee.

Obviously, as café locations go, the Piazza is unsurpassed. So are its prices, but most visitors understandably decide to splurge once at one of these famous cafés with their odd little orchestras.

Less crowded, less expensive, less beautiful but marvellously Venetian are the *campos* scattered throughout the city, each traditionally the social centre of its quarter. Try bustling San Polo on the way between the Rialto Bridge and the Frari church or the *campo* by San Stefano, not far from the Accademia Bridge.

Surprisingly, the city has rather few benches or other "free" places to sit. But you can sit down—and enjoy the greenery—in Napoleon's Public Gardens, a longish stroll or a nice *vaporetto* ride beyond St. Mark's basin, or in a tiny park between the Doges' Palace and Harry's Bar.

Harry's, a watering and victualling spot at the San Marco *vaporetto* station, has become a Venetian institution, a place (one often hears) frequented in the past by people like Hemingway and Orson Welles. It's rather small and has no outdoor seating, but for those who pay the prices, it's one of Europe's best celebrity- and aristocracy-watching establishments.

As everywhere in Italy, it costs considerably more—perhaps three times as much—to sit down and have a coffee or drink than to take it standing at the counter. But, aside from the Piazza, Venice café prices are fairly reasonable.

Nightlife

Venice has a handful of discotheques and more traditional dancing establishments, primarily patronized by young people.

The few nightclubs cater primarily for older age groups, with prices at high international levels for floor shows, dancing and dining.

Venice's casino, a municipal institution, holds forth at the Lido in spring and summer then moves to the Palazzo Vendramin Calergi on the Grand Canal for the off-sea-

After a full day of museums and churches, it's time to relax.

son months. In both locations, there are floor shows, restaurants and dancing, but the main attraction is the action: you can play roulette, chemin de fer, baccarat and black jack (21) from 3 p.m. to 3 a.m. daily, but no poker or dice (craps). Take your passport to gain admittance to the gambling rooms.

It's hard to believe about an Italian city, but Venice —home for centuries to Europe's most celebrated courtesans—has practically no prostitution today. Out-of-town practitioners may try their luck during the tourist season, but they're quickly discouraged by police. A handful of somewhat aging local ladies may be seen late at night on a walkway or two near the Piazza.

Everybody who's anybody in Venice appears at Fenice's premières.

The Arts

Now that the death-by-drowning notices for Venice have happily proved premature, cultural events are leading the city's renaissance. The year-round schedule may include excellent programmes of music, dance, theatre, cinema or art exhibitions. In odd-numbered years, the famous Biennale of Contemporary Arts is staged.

Venice's churches and neighbourhood organizations offer music and dance programmes, often foreign sponsored. Organ and choral concerts are frequently given in the basilica of San Marco. If you're lucky, they might be doing *Otello* in the courtyard of the Doges' Palace while you're in Venice.

Europe's prettiest theatre, La Fenice (The Phoenix) is naturally the focal point of musical Venice. Opera, symphonic and choral concerts, ballet and even modern dance are presented here, often to glittering audiences reminiscent of the good old days. La Fenice normally closes only in August.

Then there's the old Teatro Goldoni, now totally rebuilt, which offers a fine programme of plays year round.

To find out what's going on in Venice, look at pillars, billboards, walls and embankments for those colourful posters detailing current attractions.

Late each summer, the Venice film festival at the Lido attracts serious cinema specialists as well as the usual celebrities and would-be celebrities. It's difficult, often impossible, for ordinary tourists to see the films. Otherwise, Venice has no permanent foreign-language cinemas.

Sports

Swimming: Pessimists say that swimming will only be permitted for another few years at the Adriatic beaches near Venice, but thus far the pollution levels have not risen to danger point. The swimming season at the Lido runs from June 15 to September 15. The main, non-hotel beach areas that charge admittance offer dressing rooms or small cabins for hire, lifeguards and snack bars. But at the Alberoni end of the seven-mile-long Lido, there is a free, minimally organized beach.

Popular beaches line Caval-

History comes back to life during Venice's annual Regata Storica.

lino Peninsula *(Litorale del Cavallino)*, the less commercial mainland spur jutting out towards the Lido. Its terminal, Punta Sabbioni, may be reached by a pleasant ferry trip (lines 14 and 15) from the Riva in Venice. The free beach area, next to the Punta Sabbioni lighthouse, is relatively clean and usually less crowded than the closer, paying beaches. Bus services are also available from Punta Sabbioni to the popular Jesolo beach resort.

Boating: There's little chance of hiring even a rowing-boat within the Venice lagoon. This is because in the past too many tourists piloted boats irresponsibly in the canals. Your hotel desk-clerk may know a place where you can hire a motorboat with driver to explore the city and lagoon. For long-term visitors, there are boat clubs with enrolment and monthly subscription fees. On the Lido, small boats may be hired from the beach areas, and hotels will rent out sailing boats for excursions on the Adriatic.

Tourists with their own boats are welcome in Venetian waters, but owners should check with the Capitaneria del Porto, near Harry's Bar, about local regulations.

Fishing: Anglers can expect to catch eel, trout, carp, pike, sardines and mullet. Authorities are not very strict about seasons or licences with tourists.

Golf: An 18-hole course at Alberoni, on the Lido, is open all year round to anyone producing a membership card of any other golf club. Greens fees cost more on Sundays. If necessary, clubs are available for hire.

Tennis: On the Lido, there are public hard courts open from spring to autumn; they're especially crowded in the summer. Private courts on the Lido and at Mestre on the mainland, normally part of sporting associations, may let non-members play for a reasonable fee (your hotel should know).

Horse-riding: During the summer season, stables operate at the Lido, Punta Sabbioni and the Fusina camping ground near Marghera on the mainland.

Flying: Light planes may be hired from the Aeroclub at the small Lido airport, either for flights over Venice and the lagoon (memorable) or for trips to other spots in Italy. The cost of a 15-minute flight is surprisingly reasonable— there's even a family fare.

94

How to Get There

Fares and routes for local and international transport—whether by rail, sea, air, road or a combination of these—are constantly changing. Your travel agent should have the most up-to-date information, but the following outline will give you an idea of the various possibilities.

From Great Britain

BY AIR: There are several flights a week to Venice from London, and services from Dublin, Glasgow and Birmingham routed via London.

An Excursion fare is available for a stay of 6 days to 1 month, as well as the APEX (Advance Purchase Excursion) fare, valid 7 days to 3 months. The APEX fare must be booked and paid for one month before departure. Some airlines offer a fly/drive package that includes a hired car if two people travel together and stay at least 7 days.

Charter Flights and Package Tours: Many tour operators offer package holidays to Venice that include air flight, hotel, meals and sightseeing.

BY CAR: During the summer, when cross-Channel ferry space is at a premium, be sure you have a firm reservation. In about 35 minutes, for around the same price as the ferry, you can take the hovercraft from Ramsgate or Dover to Calais. You can follow toll motorways (expressways) through most of France to the Italian border, then continue eastward to Venice on the *autostrada*.

It's also possible for you and your car to travel by motorail from Boulogne or Paris to Milan. British Rail will have the details.

BY RAIL: Tickets from the United Kingdom to Venice are issued for a period of two months, and you may stop over along the way without formalities.

Eurailpass: North Americans—in fact, anyone except residents of Europe—can travel on a flat-rate, unlimited mileage ticket valid for first-class rail travel anywhere in Western Europe outside of Great Britain. The Eurailpass may be purchased for periods of 2 or 3 weeks, 1, 2 or 3 months. Eurail Youthpass offers second-class travel to anyone under 26. You must buy your pass before leaving home.

Inter-Rail Card: This ticket permits 30 days of unlimited rail travel in participating European countries and Morocco to people under 26 and over 65. In the country of issue, fares are given a 50% discount.

BY COACH: Europabus, the motorcoach system of the European railways, runs many buses to Italy. The principal route goes through Antwerp and Luxembourg to Aosta and Milan.

From North America

BY AIR: You can fly to London, Paris, Milan or Rome for direct, connecting flights to Venice. The usual route is via Milan.

Two bargain fares are currently available. The APEX (Advance Purchase Excursion) fare for a period of 14 to 45 days is the least expensive. Tickets must be reserved and paid for 21 days prior to departure. Children receive a 33% discount. The 14 to 120-day Excursion fare does not require advance reservation and may be booked with an open return.

Charter Flights and Package Tours: Group Inclusive Tours (GIT) last 8 days or 14–21 days, and include some part of the land programme, such as accommodation, excursions, some or all meals and transfers. Advance Booking Charters (ABC), for flight only, require that you sign up 45 days in advance and remain in Italy at least one week.

When to Go

Venice works its magic on visitors all year round, but all things considered, the best time to go is in spring or autumn. During the summer, the city is very crowded, steamy odours may rise from the canals, and prices are at their Venetian peak. In the winter, you may run into thick fog (which prompts those memorable Venetian foghorns to boom around the lagoon), high waters, cold or even snow, but there will also be many sunny days—and no crowds. The weather is most pleasant between April and June and again in September and October.

Average monthly temperatures:

		J	F	M	A	M	J	J	A	S	O	N	D
Air temperature													
Max.	°F	42	46	54	63	71	77	83	83	79	65	54	46
	°C	6	8	12	17	22	25	28	28	26	18	12	8
Min.	°F	34	34	41	51	57	64	68	66	62	52	43	37
	°C	1	1	5	10	14	18	20	19	17	11	6	3

Planning Your Budget

To give you an idea of what to expect, here are some average prices in Italian lire (L.). However, remember that all prices must be regarded as approximate and that the inflation rate is high.

Airport transfers: *public bus* from airport to Piazzale Roma L. 200, luggage charge L. 200 per bag; *airline bus* L. 1,500; *motorboat* from airport to Piazza San Marco L. 7,000; *taxi* from airport to Piazzale Roma L. 11,000.

Baby-sitters: L. 2,000–5,000 per hour.

Camping: L. 2,500 per person per night, plus L. 2,000 for tents/caravans, L.1,000 for cars.

Cigarettes (per packet of 20): Italian brands L. 800, imported L. 1,000.

Eintertainment: *cinema* L. 2,500–3,000, *discotheque* (entry and first drink) L. 5,000, *opera* L. 3,500–12,000.

Guides (1–10 persons): full day L. 60,000, half day L. 35,000.

Guided tours: Murano–Burano–Torcello L. 10,000 per person; by *burchiello* to Padua L. 40,000.

Hairdressers: shampoo and set/blow dry L.10,000, colour rinse L. 13,000. **Barbers:** haircut L. 8,000.

Hotels (double room with bath, summer season, breakfast not included): *luxury class* L. 200,000, *1st class* L. 100,000–130,000, *2nd class* L. 55,000–70,000, *3rd class* L. 37,000; youth hostels: L. 5,000 per person, breakfast included.

Meals and drinks: Continental *breakfast* L. 3,500–6,000, 3-course meal in fairly good establishment L. 12,000–20,000, *coffee* L. 600, *bottle of wine* L. 3,000 and up, *beer* L. 800, *soft drink* L. 800, *aperitif* L. 1,000.

Museums: L. 500–2,000.

Shopping bag: 500 g. of *bread* L. 1,000, 250 g. of *butter* L. 1,200, 6 eggs L. 700, 500 g. of *beefsteak* L. 6,000, 250 g. of *coffee* L. 2,000, bottle of table *wine* L. 1,000.

Transport: *vaporetto* (waterbus) any distance, one uninterrupted ride L. 500; by the fast *diretto* L. 600; *motoscafo* (water-taxi) from Piazzale Roma to San Marco L. 13,000 for up to four persons, each additional person L. 900; *gondola* L. 25,000 for 50 minutes for up to six persons.

BLUEPRINT for a Perfect Trip

An A-Z Summary of Practical Information and Facts

A star (*) following an entry indicates that relevant prices are to be found on page 97.

Listed after most entries is the appropriate Italian translation, usually in the singular, plus a number of phrases that may come in handy during your stay in Italy.

Although every effort has been made to ensure the accuracy of the information contained in this book, changes will inevitably occur, and we would be pleased to hear of any new developments.

ACCOMMODATION* (see also CAMPING). Venice's 200 places of A
lodging include the simplest inns *(locande)* as well as the most de luxe
hotels *(albergo* or *hotel)* in Europe. Advance booking is essential from
spring to autumn, and it's wise even during the winter since many
hotels close at that time. (Almost no hotels on the Lido remain open
between November and April.) At Marco Polo airport, the railway
station and Piazzale Roma, there is a hotel information and booking
service.

Room rates at hotels on the Grand Canal range from expensive
to outrageous and do not include breakfast. Still the management is
likely to urge you to have your tea and brioche or whatever on the
premises at a price many, many times what you'd pay for a *cappuccino*
and pastry at a stand-up bar.

Most 4th-class hotels, *pensione* and *locanda,* have only rooms with
hot and cold running water but it is also possible to find accommodation with bath.

Single-room prices average about 60 per cent of double rates. While
most hotels don't have formal off-season rates, you can often arrange
a lower price during the winter.

Day hotels *(albergo diurno).* Just off Piazza San Marco, by the post-
telegraph office behind the Napoleonic Wing, there is one of those
handy Italian institutions. Here, for delightfully low charges, you may
freshen up with a shower or bath, leave luggage or parcels, have a
haircut, manicure or massage or take a room for a few hours of rest.
The address is
San Marco, Ascensione 1266

Youth hostels *(ostello della gioventù).* Venice's only official youth hostel is on the island of Giudecca at
Fondamenta Zitelle, 86; tel. 38211.

It has 320 beds and is open year-round except for the period between
December 15 and February 1. This approved Youth Hostel Associa-
tion establishment is reached by *vaporetto* lines 5 or 8; otherwise, the
closest hostel is at Jesolo. The Venice Ente Provinciale per il Turismo
(see TOURIST INFORMATION OFFICES) has a list of student houses, con-
vents, etc. to which it sends young tourists during the summer.

I'd like a single/double room | **Vorrei una camera singola/matri-moniale.**

with (without) bath/shower | **con (senza) bagno/doccia**
What's the rate per night? | **Qual è il prezzo per una notte?** 99

A   **AIRPORT** *(aeroporto)*. Marco Polo di Tessera international airport lies on the mainland, 13 kilometres north of Venice. However, many European airlines do *not* fly to Venice, so ask your travel agent.

Ground transport*. Public buses run about once an hour between the airport and the Piazzale Roma car park, usually a 20-minute trip. Airline buses are more conveniently scheduled for flight departures—but they cost considerably more. Taxis are also available.

Water transportation*. Unless the lagoon is unduly choppy, motorboats ply directly between the airport and Piazza San Marco, coinciding with flight departures and arrivals. The picturesque trip takes about 30 minutes.

Check-in times. 35 minutes before international departures; 25 minutes before domestic flights. Luggage may be checked in only at the airport.

Facilities. There are porters to carry your luggage the short distance between bus or motorboat stop and check-in counters. Marco Polo airport has a small duty-free shop, a currency-exchange office *(cambio)*, a souvenir and newspaper stand, lavatories, an unexciting restaurant and welcome air-conditioning.

Domestic air travel. Alitalia, the national airline, flies from Venice to Rome and Milan. A domestic airline, Itavia, has less frequent flights to other Italian cities.

Porter!	**Facchino!**
Taxi!	**Taxi!**
Where's the boat for ...	**Dove si prende il vaporetto per ...?**
Where's the bus for ...?	**Dove si prende l'autobus per...?**

B   **BABY-SITTERS*** *(bambinaia)*. Many hotels keep lists of baby-sitters (generally students) known to them personally, and the local paper *(Il Gazzettino)* carries sitter advertisements.

Can you get me a baby-sitter for tonight?	**Può trovarmi una bambinaia per questa sera?**

BICYCLE HIRE *(noleggio biciclette)*. All wheeled transport is banned in Venice with the exception of the tiniest baby scooters or tricycles. Bicycles may be rented on the Lido and nearby mainland. Ask your

hotel receptionist or any tourist information office for the address of a
bicycle rental firm.

| I'd like to hire a bicycle. | **Vorrei noleggiare una bicicletta.** |
| What's the charge per day? | **Qual é la tariffa al giorno?** |

CAMPING* *(campeggio)*. There is no camping in Venice or on the
Lido, but campsites abound on the mainland. Around Mestre, easily
accessible by bus or train from Venice, the camping season runs from
late March until November.

The Cavallino peninsula, reached from Venice by *vaporetti* Nos. 12,
14 and 15, has well-equipped sites at Punta Sabbioni, Treporti, Lido di
Jesolo and many others further along the beach strip. The camping
season runs from April to September. Some Cavallino sites also have
bungalows (for four people, without bathing facilitics).

Other campsites are Chioggia and Sottomarina.

The Venice area campsites are listed under "Campeggi—Ostelli—
Villaggi Turistici" in the yellow pages of the telephone book.

You can also contact the Ente Provinciale per il Turismo (see
Tourist Information Offices) for a comprehensive list of sites, rates
and facilities.

In Italy, you may camp freely outside of sites if you obtain permission either from the owner of the property or from the local authori-
tics but it's wisest to chose a place where there are other campers.

If you enter Italy with a caravan (trailer) you must be able to show
an inventory (with two copies) of the material and equipment in the
caravan: dishes, linen, etc.

May we camp here?	**Possiamo campeggiare qui?**
Is there a campsite near here?	**C'è un campeggio qui vicino?**
We have a tent/caravan (trailer).	**Abbiamo la tenda/la roulotte.**

CAR HIRE *(autonoleggio)*. Major car-rental firms and scores of small
private operators vie for the tourist trade at Venice's Piazzale Roma
car park, the airport, Mestre and other nearby mainland points.
They're all listed in the yellow pages of the telephone book, and many
hotels have arrangements with an agency. A valid driving licence is
needed to hire a car, insurance is mandatory and a deposit is usually
required (except for holders of major credit cards). Minimum age
varies from 21 to 25 according to the company. Large agencies will let
you leave a rented car in another Italian or European city for an additional fee. Usually only Italian cars are available.

C

Special weekend rates and weekly unlimited-mileage rates for non-Italians may be available. In addition to regular rental agencies, there are many private car owners who chauffeur tourists to points in the Venetian hinterland. Hotels can normally arrange this, and the rates are definitely negotiable.

I'd like to rent a car ...	**Vorrei noleggiare un'automobile ...**
tomorow.	**per domani.**
for one day	**per un giorno**
for a week	**per una settimana**

CIGARETTES, CIGARS, TOBACCO★ *(sigarette, sigari, tabacco).*
Legally, tobacco products and matches in Italy may be sold only at state-controlled prices in shops bearing a large white *T* on a black background or at certain authorized hotel news-stands and café counters. Foreign brands cost as much as 50% more than domestic cigarettes. Many of the best-known foreign cigarettes, except for menthol types, are available.

It's hard to find good foreign cigars though. The Dutch, German and Italian brands available are not outstanding. The foreign pipe tobacco available in Venice, including American brands, may cost twice as much as in their country of origin.

T shops also sell lighters, postage stamps, sweets, small souvenirs and greeting cards.

I'd like a packet ...	**Vorrei un pacchetto di ...**
with/without filter	**con/senza filtro**
I'd like a box of matches.	**Per favore, mi dia una scatola di fiammiferi.**

CLOTHING. Since Venice is normally warm, hot or scorching from May to September, lightweight summer wear is in order. But evenings can be cool, so bring along a sweater or light wrap. (Something of the sort is also handy to cover bare shoulders when visiting churches.) And occasionally, even in the summer, it rains.

In late autumn, winter and early spring, Venice is often cold and damp. There may even be snow. None of this weather is as bad as that experienced north of the Alps so medium-weight clothing should suffice under a warm coat. In any season, comfortable walking shoes are indispensable. In the off-season, when parts of the city are flooded

102

by *acqua alta* (high water), many Venetians go around in knee boots. But if this happens during your visit, you can always buy a very cheap pair of boots on the spot.

Although Venice is an informal city, diners at the best restaurants do dress up a bit during the indoor season. Men wear jackets and ties and, for the fanciest receptions and premières, formal attire.

Slacks for women are acceptable everywhere, and in warm weather neither jackets nor ties are required for men. At beaches and pools, nudity is technically forbidden, but the "mini-est" of bikinis and occasional toplessness will be seen.

COMMUNICATIONS

Post offices (*posta* or *ufficio postale*) handle telegrams, mail and money transfers, and some have public telephones. Postage stamps are also sold at tobacconists (*tabaccaio*) and at some hotel desks. Post boxes are red; the slot marked *Per la città* is for Venice mail only, *Altre destinazioni* for mail going elsewhere.

Post office **hours** are normally from 8.30 a.m. to 2 p.m., Monday to Saturday.

Venice's main post office at the Rialto Bridge is open from 8.30 a.m. to 7 p.m., Monday to Saturday, but packages are accepted for mailing only until 2 p.m. The poste restante (general delivery) service functions until 5 p.m. In the lobby, telegrams, telexes, express and registered letters may be sent 24 hours a day.

The conveniently located branch just outside the Piazza closes at 2 p.m.

Poste restante (general delivery). It's not worth arranging to receive mail during a brief visit to Venice. Italy's postal system is rather unreliable. Instead, have people cable or telephone your hotel. But if you're going to be in Venice for a considerable time and must have things sent to you, there is poste restante (*fermo posta*) service at the main post office.

Don't forget your passport as identification when you go to pick up mail. Have mail adressed to you in care of:

Fermo Posta
Posta Centrale, Rialto
Venice, Italy

Telegrams (*telegramma*): Night letters, or night-rate telegrams (*lettera telegramma*), which arrive the next morning, are far cheaper than ordinary cables but can only be sent overseas.

C **Parcels** *(pacco):* Bureaucratic regulations about wrapping and sending packages from Italy—involving different classifications, sealing procedures, insurance, customs requirements, etc.—are so complicated that even immensely knowledgeable hotel concierges don't know them all. Ask at a post office.

Telephone *(telefono).* There are a few strategically placed phone booths around the city and in almost every bar and café, indicated by a sign showing a telephone dial and receiver.

In the bank of phone booths marked *Interurbane*, on the market side of the Rialto Bridge, you may dial other Italian cities directly. All public phones require tokens *(gettoni)*, which you can buy at a bar or at a machine by the booth.

And now for the fun: insert the token and lift the receiver. The normal dial tone is a series of long dash sounds, something you may not hear right away. A dot-dot-dot series means Venice's central computer is overloaded; hang up and try again. If the dot-dots interrupt when you're dialling the number, that means a district line is overloaded. Or, you may dial all the way through and hear nothing at all.

Of course, it's much easier (but also more expensive) to have your hotel receptionist put through the call, or go to the telephone office at Rialto post office (open day and night) where operators place your call. If you want to reverse the charge *(chiamata* "R"—pronounced *kyah-maa-tah ay-ray),* be prepared for a long wait.

Some useful numbers:
Venice directory inquiries (information) 12
Operator for Europe, North Africa and ships at sea 15
Operator for Western hemisphere and Asia 170
Direct dialling for Great Britain 0044

Give me ... *gettoni,* please.	**Per favore, mi dia ... gettoni.**
Can you get me this number in ...?	**Può passarmi questo numero a ...?**
Have you received any mail for ...?	**C'è posta per ...?**
I'd like a stamp for this letter/postcard.	**Desidero un francobollo per questa lettera/cartolina.**
express (special delivery)	**espresso**
airmail	**via aerea**
registered	**raccomandata**
I want to send a telegram to ...	**Desidero mandare un telegramma a ...**

COMPLAINTS *(reclamo)*. Forewarned or not, many tourists complain mightily when they encounter Venice's prices. In the rare instance of apparently criminal over-charging, misrepresenting a price or altering a bill, recourse should first be sought from the establishment's manager or proprietor. If that fails, threatening to inform the Ente Provinciale per il Turismo (see TOURIST INFORMATION OFFICES) should bring some results. Finally, for all serious complaints, including outright theft, telephone the police *questura* (see POLICE).

To avoid problems in all situations, always establish the price in advance—especially when dealing with porters at stations. If possible, leave excess bags in the left-luggage (check rooms) at either Piazzale Roma or the railway station.

CONSULATES and EMBASSIES

Australia (consulate): Via Turati, 40, Milan; tel. 6598727

Canada (consulate): Via V. Pisani, 19, Milan; tel. 652600

Eire (embassy): Via del Pozzetto, 105, Rome; tel. 6782541

South Africa (embassy): Piazza Monte Grappa, 4, Rome; tel. 3608441

United Kingdom (consulate): Dorsoduro, 1051, Venice; tel. 27207

U.S.A. (consulate): Piazza Repubblica, 32, Milan; tel. 652841

Most consulates are open from Monday to Friday from about 9 a.m. to 5 p.m., but close at lunch time.

Where is the British/American consulate?

Dov'è il consolato britannico/ americano?

CONVERTER CHARTS. For fluid, tire pressure and distance measures, see page 109. Italy uses the metric system.

Temperature

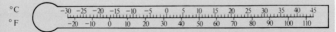

Length

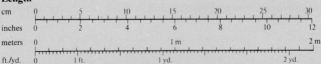

C

Weight

grams	0	100	200	300	400	500	600	700	800	900	1 kg
ounces	0	4	8	12	1 lb	20	24	28	2 lb.		

COURTESIES. See also MEETING PEOPLE. Italians practise basic social courtesies, but Venice is a relaxed, informal city. On entering and leaving a shop, restaurant or office, the usual greeting is *buon giorno* (good morning) or *buona sera* (good evening). When approaching someone with an inquiry, *per favore* is please, *grazie* is thanks, to which the reply *prego* means don't mention it or you're welcome. Introductions to men, women and older children are always accompanied by a handshake, the usual phrase being *piacere* (it's a pleasure). For "good-bye" you can use the word *arrivederci* (until we meet again) or *ciao*, which is very informal and only for those you know well.

There are two ways of saying "excuse me". If you mean "I didn't hear very well", you say *mi scusi*. "May I please get past you?" is *permesso*.

How are you?	**Come va?**
Very well, thanks.	**Molto bene, grazie.**

CRIME and THEFT. No matter what the papers say, in Venice cases of violence involving tourists are rare. Though women may be pestered, such attention is unlikely to escalate beyond acceptable bounds. Petty thieves, particularly pick-pockets, operate here as in all tourist centres. It's wise to leave your unneeded documents and excess money locked up at the hotel. Women should be aware that agile thieves may make off with their bags by cutting the shoulder straps.

In the tourist season, con-men may offer stolen goods (especially, transistors, watches, cameras) or "bargain" items which, though apparently brand new, are likely to be of extremely poor workmanship.

I want to report a theft.	**Voglio denunciare un furto.**
My wallet/handbag/passport/ ticket has been stolen.	**Mi hanno rubato il portafoglio/ la borsa/il passaporto/il biglietto.**

CUSTOMS *(dogana)* **and ENTRY REGULATIONS.** For a stay of up to three months, a valid passport is sufficient for citizens of Australia, Canada, New Zealand and U.S.A. Visitors from Eire and the United

Kingdom need only an identity card to enter Italy. Tourists from South Africa must have a visa.

Italian customs officials are unlikely to quibble over smaller points: they are interested mainly in detecting smuggled art treasures, currency or narcotics. If you're exporting archaeological relics, works of art, or gems, you should obtain a bill of sale and a permit from the government (this is normally handled by the dealer).

Here's what you can take into Italy duty-free and, when returning home, into your own country:

Entering Italy from:	Cigarettes		Cigars		Tobacco	Spirits		Wine
1)	200	or	50	or	250 g.	³/₄ l.	or	2 l.
2)	300	or	75	or	400 g.	1.5 l.	or	3 l.
3)	400		100		500 g.	³/₄ l.		2 l.
Into:								
Australia	200	or	250 g.	or	250 g.	1 l.	or	1 l.
Canada	200	and	50	and	900 g.	1.1 l.	or	1.1 l.
Eire	200	or	50	or	250 g.	1 l.	and	2 l.
N. Zealand	200	or	50	or	½ lb.	1 qt.	and	1 qt.
S. Africa	400	and	50	and	250 g.	1 l.	and	1 l.
U.K.	200	or	50	or	250 g.	1 l.	and	2 l.
U.S.A.	200	and	100	and	4)	1 l.	or	1 l.

1) within Europe from non-EEC countries
2) within Europe from EEC countries
3) countries outside Europe
4) a reasonable quantity

Currency restrictions. Non-residents may import or export up to L. 200,000 in local currency. In foreign currencies, tourists may import unlimited amounts, but to take the equivalent of more than L. 200,000 back out of Italy, you must present a V2 declaration form (filled out upon entry) at the border.

I've nothing to declare.   **Non ho nulla da dichiarare.**
It's for personal use.   **È per mio uso personale.**

D   **DRIVING IN ITALY**

Entering Italy: To bring your car into Italy, you will need:

- an International Driving Licence or a valid national licence
- car registration papers
- Green Card (an extension to your regular insurance policy, making it valid for foreign countries). Though not obligatory for EEC countries, it's still preferable to have it.
- a red warning triangle in case of breakdown
- national identity sticker for your car

Driving conditions: Traffic on major roads has right of way over traffic entering from side-roads, but this, like other traffic regulations, is frequently ignored, so beware. At intersections of roads of similar importance, the car on the right theoretically has the right of way. When passing other vehicles, or remaining in the left-hand (passing) lane, keep your directional indicator flashing.

The expressways *(autostrada)* are designed for fast and safe driving: each section requires the payment of a toll: you collect a card from an automatic machine or from the booth attendant and pay at the other end for the distance travelled. Try to stock up on 100-lira coins and small banknotes, since the toll booth attendants don't like making change. There's often a lane on the extreme right for slow traffic.

Last but not least: cars, buses, lorries (trucks) make use, indiscriminately, of their horns. In fact, blowing one's horn is an Italian attitude, so don't get flustered if it's done at you, and blow your own horn whenever it could help to warn of your impending arrival.

Speed limits. Speed limits in Italy are based on the car engine size. The following chart gives the engine size in cubic centimetres and the limits (in kilometres per hour) on the motorway:

Engine size	less than 600 cc.	600 to 900 cc.	900 to 1300 cc. (and motorcycles more than 150 cc.)	more than 1300 cc.
Main roads	80 kph.	90 kph.	100 kph.	110 kph.
Motorways (Expressways)	90 kph.	110 kph.	130 kph.	140 kph.

108

Town speed limits are posted on the entry roads in kilometres per hour.

Traffic police *(polizia stradale):* When seen—not very often—Italian traffic police use motorcycles or Alfa-Romeos, usually light blue. All cities and many towns and villages have signs posted at the outskirts indicating at least the telephone number of the local traffic police or the *carabinieri.* Speeding fines can often be paid on the spot, but ask for a receipt *(ricevuta).*

Breakdowns: Garages are everywhere in Italy. Mechanics are willing if not always able to handle your problem, and major towns have agencies specializing in foreign cars. You can dial 116 for emergency service from the Automobile Club d'Italia. Call boxes are located at regular intervals on the *autostrade* in case of breakdowns or other emergencies.

Fuel and oil: Service stations abound in Italy, most with at least one mechanic on duty (who's likely to be a Fiat specialist but a bit vague about foreign cars). Fuel *(benzina),* sold at government-set prices, comes in regular *(normale)* of 84 octane and extra *(super)* of 98 octane. Diesel fuel is usually also available. The petrol price has risen repeatedly so that it is now about the highest in Europe.

Fluid measures

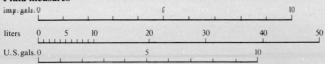

To help you convert kilometres to miles:

Parking: The Piazzale Roma, the closest you can get to central Venice by car, has two large, multi-level garages. However, a huge car park exists on the adjacent island of Tronchetto, connected from May to October by public water-bus service *(motoscafo* No. 3) to the centre of the city. From Tronchetto there is also a frequent car-ferry service to the Lido where cars are permitted and where parking is usually possible. The two new car parks at Mestre, San Giuliano and Fusina, can be reached directly from Venice (June to September) by *(vaporetto).*

D Although the outdoor car parks near Venice are supposedly guarded night and day—a service for which you are charged—don't leave anything valuable inside your car, even if you lock it and take the key. In the garages, you must leave your doors open and the key in the ignition. There are left-luggage (baggage-check) facilities, including lockers, at Piazzale Roma.

Road Signs. Most road signs employed in Italy are international pictographs, but here are some written ones you might come across:

Accendre le luci	Use headlights
Deviazione	Diversion (Detour)
Divieto di sorpasso	No overtaking (passing)
Divieto di sosta	No stopping
Lavori in corso	Road works (Men working)
Passaggio a livello	Level railway crossing
Pericolo	Danger
Rallentare	Slow down
Senso vietato/unico	No entry/One-way street
Vietato l'ingresso	No entry
Zona pedonale	Pedestrian zone

(International) Driving Licence	**patente (internazionale)**
car registration papers	**libretto di circolazione**
Green Card	**carta verde**

Finally, some expressions that could be useful:

Where's the nearest car park?	**Dov'è il parcheggio più vicino?**
Can I park here?	**Posso parcheggiare qui?**
Are we on the right road for ...?	**Siamo sulla strada giusta per ...?**
Fill the tank please, top grade.	**Per favore, faccia il pieno di super.**
Check the oil/tires/battery.	**Controlli l'olio/i pneumatici/ la batteria.**
I've had a breakdown.	**Ho avuto un guasto.**
There's been an accident.	**C'è stato un incidente.**

DRUGS. Anyone possessing or selling drugs in Italy faces an unusually aroused police force and extremely severe legal penalties. No distinction is made between soft and hard drugs. Present maximum sentence is about eight years in prison and/or extremely stiff fines.

In every sense, drugs are a huge risk in Italy. Because of the monumental backlog in the nation's court cases, a person arrested on suspicion of a narcotics crime may spend as long as one year in jail before even being formally charged. Foreign consulates and embassies advise their citizens that there is no way for them to speed up the legal process.

ELECTRIC CURRENT *(elettricità)*. Electricity of 220 volts is supplied in all but a few very old areas of Venice. Non-Italian electric appliances may require a special adaptor plug to fit local sockets.

What's the voltage, 220 or 110?	**Qual è il voltaggio, 220 (duecentoventi) o 110 (centodieci)?**
I'd like an adaptor/ a battery.	**Vorrei una presa complementare/ una batteria.**

EMERGENCIES. A local resident who can speak enough English to help out in an emergency is almost always close at hand in Venice. If not, the main numbers to call are:

Police, all-purpose emergency number	113
Carabinieri (see POLICE) for urgent police problems	3 22 22
Ambulance, first-aid	3 00 00 or 70 56 22
Fire	2 22 22/3
Assistance on the road—A.C.I.	116

Depending on the nature of the problem, see also separate entries on CONSULATES, MEDICAL CARE, POLICE, etc.

Ambulances and fire engines are boats. On every *vaporetto*, signs (in Italian) tell you what to do in emergencies. Sirens will sound if there is a person overboard or a fire; anyone who sees a person fall overboard must shout *"uomo in mare!"* and, of course, throw in the nearest lifebelt; for a fire, you will hear *"incendio!"* and if the boat is in peril, *"abbandono nave!"*

Careful!	**Attenzione!**	Police!	**Polizia!**
Fire!	**Incendio!**	Stop!	**Stop!**
Help!	**Aiuto!**	Stop thief!	**Al ladro!**

Please, can you place an emergency call for me to the ...?	**Per favore, può fare per me una telefonata d'emergenza ....?**
police	**alla polizia**
fire brigade	**ai pompieri**
hospital	**all'ospedale**

111

G   **GUIDES** *(guida)* **and TOURS*.** Your hotel should be able to arrange for an experienced guide to accompany you in Venice. At most major tourist attractions you'll find coin-operated machines, some equipped with coloured slides, which provide taped descriptions of what you're seeing—in four or five languages.

The Italian tourist agency, CIT, and about two dozen private firms offer guided tours on foot and by boat within Venice and the lagoon, and by bus or limousine to the Veneto region on the mainland. Farther afield, there are commercial tours available to Yugoslavia, the north Italian lake district, Ravenna and Florence. Travel agencies in Venice's hotel areas advertise a wide variety of excursions, and hotels have lists of tours for their clients.

We'd like an English-speaking guide.	**Desideriamo una guida che parla inglese.**
I need an English interpreter.	**Ho bisogno di un interprete d'inglese.**

H   **HAIRDRESSERS and BARBERS*** *(parrucchiere, barbiere).* Italian hairdressers deserve their reputation for excellence. Men will find professional and speedy service in Venice; women will be wise to call ahead for an appointment. Prices in the Piazza San Marco are markedly higher than elsewhere in town. It's customary to tip a barber 10–15%. Ladies should not tip the owner of a salon, but the shampooer, manicurist or stylist should receive up to 15% of the bill. Hairdressers may have facilities for facial treatments, make-up and massage.

I'd like a shampoo and set.	**Vorrei shampo e messa in piega.**
I want a ...	**Voglio ...**
haircut	**il taglio**
shave	**la rasatura**
blow-dry	**asciugatura al fon**
colour rinse	**un riflesso**
manicure	**la manicure**
Don't cut it too short.	**Non li tagli troppo corti.**
A little more off (here).	**Un po' di più (qui).**

HITCH-HIKING *(autostop).* There's not much hope of hitch-hiking around Venice's canals and lagoon: gondoliers don't give free lifts and it's unlikely that a cement scow or ironmongers' barge will take you aboard. On *terraferma* (Venice's term for the mainland), hitch-hiking is allowed in Italy, except on motorways, where prominent *no autostop* signs are posted at entrances to the *autostrade*. Every summer thousands of young people hitch rides all over the country, including from Piazzale Roma. A girl alone should definitely not hitch-hike; travelling in pairs is wiser.

Can you give me a lift to ...?   **Può darmi un passaggio fino a ...?**

HOURS (see also COMMUNICATIONS, MONEY MATTERS and PUBLIC HOLIDAYS). On all national holidays, banks, government offices, most shops and some museums and galleries are closed.

Shops. Open 9 a.m. 12.30 p.m. and 4 p.m.–8 p.m., Monday to Saturday from June to September. Off-season hours are 9 a.m. 12.30 p.m. and 3 p.m.–7 p.m. Monday to Saturday. *N.B.* All shops are closed on Monday mornings *except* food stores, which close on Wednesday afternoons.

Museums[*]

Accademia. 9 a.m.–2 p.m., closed Mondays.

Collezione Guggenheim. 2 p.m.–7 p.m., closed Tuesdays. April to October only.

Museo Storico Navale. 9 a.m.–1 p.m., closed Sundays.

Palazzo Ducale. 8.30 a.m.–6 p.m. daily from June to September, 9 a.m.–4 p.m. off-season.

Palazzo Rezzonico. 10 a.m.–4 p.m., closed on Friday and on Saturday afternoons.

Scuola di San Giorgio degli Schiavoni. 10 a.m.–12.30 p.m. and 3–6 p.m., closed Mondays.

Scuola Grande di San Rocco. 9 a.m.–12.30 p.m. and 3.30–6 p.m.; November to April, mornings only.

Churches generally close at lunch time. They may not be visited during religious services.

Basilica of San Marco is open daily from early morning until at least nightfall. Pala d'Oro and the treasury may be visited from 9.30 a.m.–4.30 p.m., on Sundays from 2–4.30 p.m.

Are you open tomorrow?   **È aperto domani?**

L **LANGUAGE.** It's an unusual Venice hotel that has only Italian-speaking staff. Normally the personnel know at least enough workable English, French and German to be helpful. In shops around the Piazza and the Rialto, you should have no language problems, but elsewhere in the city you might get a chance to try out your Italian or resort to sign language. Italians appreciate your efforts with their language, and Venetians will forgive your confusion with their particular dialect. It even gives peninsular Italians trouble.

In Italian it's important to remember that the letter "c" is often pronounced like "ch"—when it is followed by an "e" or "i"—while the letters "ch" together sound like the "c" in cat. Thus *cento* (hundred) comes out as CHEHN-toa but *conto* (check) is pronounced KOAN-toa and *chiesa* (church), KYAI-zah.

The Berlitz phrase book ITALIAN FOR TRAVELLERS covers all situations you're likely to encounter. The Berlitz Italian-English/English-Italian pocket dictionary contains 12,500 words, plus a menu-reader supplement.

Do you speak English?	**Parla inglese?**
I don't speak Italian.	**Non parlo italiano.**

LAUNDRY and DRY-CLEANING *(lavanderia; tintoria)*. Venice has only a handful of laundromats and dry cleaners, but they're worth seeking out because hotels charge extremely high prices for such services. The yellow pages list addresses of establishments under "Lavanderia" and "Tintoria", or your hotel receptionist will tell you where the nearest facilities are to be found. The prices at a launderette are the same whether you do the job yourself or leave it with an attendant.

When will it be ready?	**Quando sarà pronto?**
I must have this for tomorrow morning.	**Mi serve per domani mattina.**

LOST PROPERTY. Venetians are noted for their honesty, and your lost property is quite likely to turn up. Restaurants will almost certainly have your forgotten camera or guidebook waiting for you at their cash desk. If you think you lost something on a *vaporetto*, there's an "Objects Found" *(Oggetti rinvenuti)* office of the water-transport agency, the ACTV at

114 St. Angelo stop (No. 9) on the Grand Canal.

Venice's general lost-property office is called the Ufficio all'Econo-
mato and is situated near the Rialto Bridge: .

Calle Corner Piscopia e Loredan

Lost children. If you lose a child in Venice, don't worry. Like all Italians, Venetians adore children, and someone will unquestionably take
doting care of your youngster on the way to the nearest police station.
You should telephone the all-purpose emergency number 113.

I've lost my wallet/handbag.   **Ho perso il portafoglio/la bor-
                                       setta.**

MAPS. Maps of Venice are on sale around the city—detailed canal
and street maps, nautical charts of the lagoon or the "monumental"
type, featuring sketches of major palaces and churches. The tourist
offices provide free, reasonably useful maps indicating the *vaporetti*
routes.

The maps in this guide were prepared by Falk-Verlag, Hamburg,
which also publishes a complete map of Italy.

a street plan of ...   **una piantina di ...**
a road map of this region   **una carta stradale di questa
                               regione**

MEDICAL CARE. If your health-insurance policy does not cover hospital bills in foreign countries, you can take out a special short-term
policy before leaving home. Visitors from Great Britain have the right
to claim public health services available to Italians, since both countries are members of the E.E.C. Before leaving home get a copy of the
proper form from the Department of Health and Social Security.

At least half a dozen Venetian doctors speak English; your hotel
will have a list. The main Venice hospital is next to the church of Ss.
Giovanni e Paolo (San Zanipolo). The number of the first-aid section
(pronto soccorso) is 705622.

The other major general hospital is in Mestre, Via Circonvalla-
zione, 50

For an ambulance, telephone 300000. Other emergency telephone
numbers are listed under the heading EMERGENCIES.

Chemists' shops, or pharmacies *(farmacia)*, are open during normal
business hours. Nights and holidays, they are open on a rotating basis,

M and the schedule is posted on every *farmacia* door and listed in the Venice newspaper *Il Gazzettino* under "Farmacie di Turno". If you're taking any unusual medication, it's best to bring along an adequate supply.

I need a doctor/a dentist.	**Ho bisogno di un medico/ dentista.**
I've a pain here.	**Ho un dolore qui.**
a stomach ache	**il mal di stomaco**
a fever	**la febbre**
a sunburn/sunstroke	**una scottatura di sole/un colpo di sole**

MEETING PEOPLE. Although Venetians proudly stress their differences from Italians, the city's young and not-so-young men still pursue foreign female visitors—but perhaps with more discretion. And they will flirt just about anywhere—on a *vaporetto*, at the top of a campanile or in museums. Favourite local techniques include offering a guided tour of a church, an effusive string of compliments, taking a girl's picture with the Piazza's pigeons, bargains in a relative's boutique or even a gondola ride. Those who are not interested should silently ignore any approach, however persistent. To start talking, even rudely, is considered a sign of encouragement.

Few Venetian girls are socially available to foreign men, but the many Italian girls who come to Venice as tourists may feel sufficiently "liberated" to accept an invitation for a drink or dinner. At cafés and discotheques, and certainly in the Piazza, you're likely to see Italian girls in pairs or trios. Though English (or French) is taught at Italian schools, you may find you have a communication problem if you don't know Italian.

MONEY MATTERS

Currency. The *lira* (plural: *lire*, abbreviated *L.* or *Lit.*) is Italy's monetary unit.

Coins: L.10, 20, 50, 100 and 200

Banknotes: L.500, 1,000, 2,000, 5,000, 10,000, 20,000, 50,000 and 100,000.

The L.10,000 and 20,000 banknotes look very much alike, so pay attention to the denomination of your currency during all transactions.

For currency restrictions, see CUSTOMS AND ENTRY REGULATIONS.

Banks *(banca)* are open from 8.30 a.m. to 1.30 p.m. (11.30 a.m. on local "semi-holidays"), Monday to Friday. They close on public holidays and weekends.

Currency exchange offices *(cambio)* reopen after the siesta, usually until at least 6.30 p.m.; some are open on Saturday. Though the currency exchange office at the railway station claims that it operates very day in summer season from 8.30 a.m. to 7 p.m., you may find it closed Sunday afternoons or after 6 p.m. on other days.

Exchange rates for hard currency are never as good at a *cambio* as at the bank—but you'll do much better than at your hotel. Passports are sometimes required when exchanging money.

Credit cards and traveller's cheques. Major hotels, many shops and some restaurants in the San Marco area and on the Lido take credit cards. Traveller's cheques are accepted almost everywhere, but it's much better to exchange your cheques for lira at a bank or *cambio*. In Venice, you don't generally get a discount on purchases paid for with traveller's cheques. Passports are required when cashing cheques.

Eurocheques are easily cashed in Italy.

Prices. Italy's galloping inflation has finally slowed to a canter, but Venice remains neck and neck with New York, Paris and Zurich in the price sweepstakes.

Within the city, thrifty citizens claim they would never make a purchase in the Piazza San Marco area. Entrance fees to most Venice sights are a bargain, as are the *vaporetti*. Gondolas and nightclubs are not. The tourist's basic expenses—accommodation, food and drink—will cost 20–30% more in Venice than in Rome. Certain prices are listed on page 97 to give you a relative idea of what things cost.

I want to change some pounds/ dollars.	**Desidero cambiare delle sterline/ dei dollari.**
Do you accept traveller's cheques?	**Accetta traveller's cheques?**
Can I pay with this credit card?	**Posso pagare con la carta di credito?**
How much is this?	**Quanto costa questo?**

NEWSPAPERS and MAGAZINES *(giornale; rivista)*. Some British and Continental newspapers, including the Paris *International Herald Tribune*, are on sale at the airport, the railway station and at news-

N stands near the Rialto Bridge and the Piazza. Foreign papers usually reach Venice a day late, but Rome's English-language *Daily American* arrives the same day. Non-Italian magazines are invariably late on Venice news-stands. Prices are high for all foreign publications, particularly the heavy London Sunday newspapers and European weeklies.

Have you any English-language newspapers?	**Avete giornali in inglese?**

P **PHOTOGRAPHY.** If you've never taken a snapshot, you'll be highly tempted to begin in Venice. The city, of course, offers all manner of compelling photo opportunities, its famous light reflected off the Adriatic and the lagoon lending marvellous finesse to colour shots. The Venetian skyline at sundown is often spectacular. Surprisingly, one can photograph with normal flash inside most churches and galleries, though special permission must be obtained to use professional lights on certain paintings.

Major brands of film are available in Venice at somewhat higher prices. It's best to take your film home or to a larger city for developing and printing.

I'd like a film for this camera.	**Vorrei una pellicola per questa macchina.**
a black and white film	**una pellicola in bianco e nero**
a colour-slide film	**una pellicola di diapositive**
a film for colour prints	**una pellicola per fotografie a colori**
35-mm film	**una pellicola trentacinque millimetri**
super-8	**super otto**
How long will it take to develop this film?	**Quanto tempo ci vuole per sviluppare questa pellicola?**
May I take a picture?	**Posso fare una fotografia?**

POLICE (*polizia, carabinieri*). Though there don't seem to be many of them, Venice's policemen function efficiently and courteously with foreign visitors. For information or directions, ask for *vigili urbani;* for minor police matters, telephone central headquarters (*questura*).

Outside of towns, the *Polizia Stradale* patrol the highways and byways (see under DRIVING).

For anything serious, telephone the *carabinieri* (military police). On the telephone, police switchboards will often be able to find someone who speaks some English, German or French.

Some police telephone numbers:

Vigili Urbani	2 40 63
Questura	70 32 22
Carabinieri	3 22 22

There's also the all-purpose emergency number, 113, which will get you police assistance.

Where's the nearest police station?	**Dov'è il più vicino posto di polizia?**

PUBLIC HOLIDAYS *(festa)*. Italy has 9 national holidays a year. When one falls on a Thursday or a Tuesday, many Italians automatically make a *ponte* (bridge) to the weekend, meaning that Friday or Monday is taken off as well.

January 1	*Capodanno* or *Primo dell'Anno*	New Year's Day
April 25	*Festa della Liberazione*	Liberation Day
May 1	*Festa del Lavoro*	Labour Day (May Day)
August 15	*Ferragosto*	Assumption Day
November 1	*Ognissanti*	All Saints' Day
December 8	*Immacolata Concezione*	Immaculate Conception
December 25	*Natale*	Christmas Day
December 26	*Santo Stefano*	St. Stephen's Day
Movable Date	*Lunedì di Pasqua (Pasquetta)*	Easter Monday

For Venetians, **Festa della Salute,** November 21, is a local holiday (see p. 65), and many small shops close for the entire day while others open only in the morning.

On the third Saturday night of July, Venice celebrates the **Festa del Redentore** (Feast Day of the Redeemer) with a fireworks display and boat serenade procession across the Giudecca Canal to the Church of the Redeemer. Sometimes a bridge of boats is built across the canal for this celebration, which marks the end of a plague in 1576.

P   On the first Sunday in September, the beloved **Regata Storica** (Historical Regatta) is staged, a marvellously colourful Grand Canal procession of boats and barges with a make-believe doge and costumed republican nobles. Then comes the Regata Sportiva, a fiercely fought racing competition between different classes of gondolas.

Note: on all national holidays, banks, government offices, most shops and some museums and galleries are closed. In Venice, the August Ferragosto holiday does not—as in many other Italian cities—occasion a week-long shutdown.

R   **RADIO and TV** *(radio; televisione).* During the tourist season, RAI, the Italian state radio and TV network, occasionally broadcasts news in English, predominantly about Italian affairs. Vatican Radio carries foreign-language religious news programmes at various times during the day. Shortwave radio reception in Venice is excellent throughout the night and part of the day. British (BBC), American (VOA) and Canadian (CBC) programmes are easily obtained on modest transistor radios. After dark, the American Armed Forces Network (AFN) from Frankfurt or Munich can be heard on regular AM radio (middle or medium wave). RAI television broadcasts only in Italian.

RELIGIOUS SERVICES *(funzione religiosa).* Roman Catholic mass in Venice's churches is normally celebrated only in Italian, but confessions are heard every day in English, French, German and Spanish at the basilica of San Marco during the tourist season. Masses are said every morning at the basilica from 7 a.m. until about 1 p.m. and again each evening, usually at 6.45.

Non-Catholic churches (Sunday services):

Anglican, Church of St. George, Dorsoduro, Campo S. Vio

Evangelical Lutheran, Cannaregio, Campo Ss. Apostoli, 4443

Evangelical Valdesian, Palazzo Cavagnis, S.ta Maria Formosa, 5170

Greek Orthodox, Castello, Calle dei Greci, 3419

Synagogue, Cannaregio, Ghetto Vecchio 1228

What time is mass/the service?   **A che ora è la messa/la funzione?**
Is it in English?   **È in inglese?**

120

SIESTA. Following hallowed Mediterranean tradition, Venice pretty effectively shuts down from June to September between 12.30 and 4 p.m. for a long lunch and a nap. (The rest of the year the siesta ends an hour earlier.) Few museums, churches or galleries are open during this time, but bars and cafés operate, and restaurants permit customers to linger at table past 3. The on-duty *farmacie* operate drowsily, the *vaporetti* seem to run somewhat fitfully, and the narrow canals resound with countless contented snores.

TIME DIFFERENCES. Italy follows Central European Time (GMT +1), and from late March to September clocks are put one hour ahead (= GMT + 2).

Summer time chart:

New York	London	**Italy**	Jo'burg	Sydney	Auckland
6 a.m.	11 a.m.	**noon**	noon	8 p.m.	10 p.m.

What time is it? **Che ore sono?**

TIPPING. Be reassured that tipping in Venice is perfectly acceptable behaviour. Many Italians who work in service jobs could not survive without these extras.

Though a 12 to 15% service charge is added on most restaurant bills, it is customary to leave an additional tip of about 5%.

The beginning of wisdom in Venice is to tip your hotel concierge when you arrive, the amount depending entirely on the category of the establishment, how long you'll stay and what kind of special service you may require. Venetian concierges, widely admired for their knowledge of the city's past and present, can prove helpful in countless and unexpected ways.

Don't tip sales personnel in shops or crewmen aboard *vaporetti*. Do tip, modestly, the elderly gondolier posted at landing stations who helps you in and out of a younger poler's craft. Always leave small change (or telephone tokens) on the counter of a bar with your cashier's ticket for coffee, ice-cream, a sandwich or whatever. Venetian tour guides may be tipped discreetly at the end of an excursion.

In public toilets, if there is an attendant, or if hand-towels and soap are used, a small tip is in order.

T Follow the chart below for rough guidelines.

Hotel porter, per bag	L. 400–500
Bellboy, errand	L. 1,000
Maid, per day	L. 1,000
Doorman, hails gondolier	L. 400–500
Tourist guide	10%
Hairdresser, Barber	See p. 112 for details
Cinema usher	L. 300
Hat check	L. 500
Lavatory attendant	L. 300

TOILETS. Most museums and galleries, but few churches, have public toilets. Restaurants, bars, cafés, large stores, the airport, railway station and car park all have facilities. For a small charge, you may also use the public toilets at the *albergo diurno* just off Piazza San Marco (see ACCOMMODATION).

Toilets may be labelled with symbols of a man or women or the initials W.C., sometimes the wording will be in Italian—*Uomini* (men) or *Donne* (women). The most confusing label for foreigners is *Signori* (men—with a final *i*) and Signore (women—with a final *e*).

Where are the toilets? **Dove sono i gabinetti?**

TOURIST INFORMATION OFFICES. The Italian State Tourist Offices (*Ente Nazionale Italiano per il Turismo*, abbreviated E.N.I.T.) are found in Italy and abroad. They publish detailed brochures with up-to-date information on accommodation, means of transport and other general tips and useful addresses for the whole country.

Italian State Tourist Offices:

Australia and New Zealand. E.N.I.T., c/o Alitalia, 118 Alfred Street, Milson Point 2061, Sydney; tel. 922-1555

Canada. 3, Place Ville-Marie, Suite 22, Montreal 113, Que.; tel. (514) 866-7667

Eire. 47, Merrion Square, Dublin 2; tel. (01) 66397

South Africa. E.N.I.T., London House, 21 Loveday Street, P.O. Box 6507, Johannesburg; tel. 838-3247

United Kingdom. 201, Regent Street, London W1R 8AY; tel. (01) 439-2311

U.S.A. 500 N. Michigan Avenue, Chicago, Il 60611; tel. (312) 644-0990

630 Fifth Avenue, New York, NY 10020; tel. (212) 245-4822

St. Francis Hotel, 360 Post Street, San Francisco, CA 94108; tel. (415) 392-6206

E.P.T. *(Ente Provinciale per il Tourismo)* **offices in Venice:**

San Marco, Ascensione 71/F; tel. 2 63 56
Piazzale Roma; tel. 2 74 02
Stazione S.ta Lucia (railway station); tel. 71 50 16

Where's the tourist office?   **Dov'è l'ufficio turistico?**

TRANSPORT. In Venice proper, of course, there's no way to move on wheels: no buses, taxis, trams, underground trains, elevated trains or even horse-drawn carriages. Instead, for public transport there are 130 diesel-motored water-buses of various descriptions, motorboat taxis and gondolas.

Waterbuses* *(vaporetto* and the smaller, faster *motoscafo)* ply the Grand Canal and shuttle to-and-from between the islands. Operated by the ACTV (Azienda del Corsorzio Trasporti Veneziani), the *vaporetti* are still a great bargain considering the scenery. The trip from the Piazzale Roma car park (or the railway station) to San Marco on the *motoscafo* No. 2, the fast *diretto*, takes no more than 20 minutes even when traffic is heavy. A cross-canal ferry is called a *traghetto*.

Water taxis* *(motoscafo di nolo)*. There are about ten motorboat-taxi stations in Venice. Their fares vary according to the pilot—his mood and assessment of your ability to pay—although theoretically the rates are fixed.

Gondolas*. Venice still has about 450 gondolas and 12 permanent gondola stations *(imbarcadero)*. Gondoliers generally remain at the same base throughout their careers.

Steamers tie up at the Statione Marittima (Zattere) or along the Riva degli Schiavoni.

T **Trains** *(treno).* Italian trains normally run on time as advertised, but in view of the predilection for names suggesting swiftness, consult the following list before choosing your train.

TEE	The international Trans Europ Express, first class only with surcharge; seat reservations essential.
Rapido	The best, fastest (and most expensive) train, which may be one-class (de-luxe/first) with all seats reserved and for which a sizable supplement may be charged.
Direttissimo or *Express*	Stops at major cities only; has both first- and second-class coaches (seat reservations are possible in first and second class).
Diretto	Slower than the *direttissimo*, it makes a number of local stops; first- and second-class coaches.
Locale	A local train which stops at almost every station.

Tickets must be purchased and reservations made at the main Santa Lucia railway station on the Grand Canal (Ferrovia *vaporetto* stop). If you lack a reservation it's wise to arrive at the station at least half an hour before departure time to ensure getting a seat. Italy's trains are often very crowded.

Where's the nearest waterbus station?	**Dov'è l'imbarcadero del vaporetto più vicino?**
When's the next waterbus/train to …?	**Quando parte il prossimo vaporetto/treno per …?**
I want a ticket to …	**Vorrei un biglietto per …**
single (one-way)	**andata**
return (round-trip)	**andata e ritorno**
first/second class	**prima/seconda classe**
Will you tell me when to get off?	**Può dirmi quando devo scendere?**
What's the fare to …?	**Qual è la tariffa per …?**

W **WATER** *(acqua).* Venice's water is perfectly safe to drink, and everyone does. With meals, however, the usual custom is to have bottled mineral water (and wine, of course), rather than tap water. Expert opinion is divided over the alleged medical wonders of mineral water, but doctors agree it doesn't do you any harm. If you meet slender Venetians who consume large portions of rice or pasta twice a day, don't be surprised if they claim that drinking two or three litres of *acqua minerale* keeps them in shape. It's a national obsession. As for tap water, if it's not drinkable, there will be a sign reading *acqua non potabile*.

a bottle of mineral water	**una bottiglia di acqua minerale**
carbonated	**gasata**
still	**naturale**

SOME USEFUL EXPRESSIONS

yes/no	**sì/no**
please/thank you	**per favore/grazie**
excuse me/you're welcome	**mi scusi/prego**
where/when/how	**dove/quando/come**
how long/how far	**quanto tempo/quanto dista**
yesterday/today/tomorrow	**ieri/oggi/domani**
day/week/month/year	**giorno/settimana/mese/anno**
left/right	**sinistra/destra**
up/down	**su/giù**
good/bad	**buono/cattivo**
big/small	**grande/piccolo**
cheap/expensive	**buon mercato/caro**
hot/cold	**caldo/freddo**
old/new	**vecchio/nuovo**
open/closed	**aperto/chiuso**
free (vacant)/occupied	**liberto/occupato**
near/far	**vicino/lontano**
early/late	**presto/tardi**
full/empty	**pieno/vuoto**
Does anyone here speak English?	**C'è qualcuno qui che parla inglese?**
I don't understand.	**Non capisco.**
Please write it down.	**Lo scriva, per favore.**
Waiter/Waitress, please.	**Cameriere!/Cameriera!** (or **Senta!** = "listen")
I'd like …	**Vorrei …**
How much is that?	**Quant'è?**

Index

An asterisk (*) next to a page number indicates a map reference. For index to Practical Information, see p. 98.